CRAVED

CRAVED

THE SECRET SAUCE TO BUILDING A
HIGHLY-SUCCESSFUL, *STANDOUT* BRAND

KELI HAMMOND

This book is intended to provide complete and accurate information on its subject matter. However, the reader is advised and cautioned that by publishing this book, the author and publisher are not providing legal, accounting, or other professional services or advice. If professional assistance is required, the services of an appropriate, qualified professional should be sought. The advice and strategies contained herein may not be suitable for every situation. The fact that an organization or corporation is referred to in this work as a citation/or potential source does not mean that the author endorses the information the organization or their website provides or the recommendations they may make.

The author has made diligent efforts to include Internet addresses that are accurate at the time of publication; however, neither the author nor publisher is responsible for inaccurate or incomplete addresses, or for changes occurring after the book was printed and published. Moreover, the author and publisher have no control over any such third-party internet sites or the content contained thereon.

In order to protect the privacy of some individuals, some names and identifying details have been changed.

Cover and interior design by RAM Creates.

ISBN: 978-1-7335807-1-7

Published and printed in the United States of America.

This book is dedicated to all the dreamers.
Keep believing, keep pushing forward,
and most importantly, never stop dreaming.

CONTENTS

PART 3 — The Key Ingredients in the Secret-Sauce

How to Read This Book

For just a moment, forget about yourself.

Forget about *your brand vision*, and forget about *your brand goals.*

Forget about making a profit, gaining influence, getting more website visits, attracting new leads and customers, expanding to new markets, seeing more social media likes and comments, and finding more opportunities.

This isn't about you or your brand.

Good marketing never centers around you.

Never.

It's always about **them.**

Always.

About.

Them.

Always.

But, who is "them?" Them is....everyone. Everyone you're trying to persuade and everyone you're trying to convince. Everyone you'd like to support you, your services, your offerings, your products, or your cause; that's who *them* is.

FROM THIS DAY FORWARD, THINK OF YOUR BRAND ONLY AS A VESSEL

A vessel that helps other people feel better, smile or enjoy life more, overcome challenges or obstacles, or see the world differently. **The first step to building a successful brand lies in understanding that good marketing never centers around you.** This principle holds true regardless of whether you're looking to develop a credible personal brand or embark on a notable entrepreneurial venture.

Removing yourself as the *focus* of your marketing will create a more solid foundation for you to build on. Also, from here on out, don't think about marketing as selling. Marketing is *not* selling. They're often confused as one and the same, but really, marketing consists of all the things you do to open the door to getting sales (without being salesy). When effective, people tend to respond much more favorably to marketing than they do to sales.

Marketing is about *attracting* people to you. So, moving forward, start to reframe everything you think you know about marketing, and instead, look at marketing as one thing, and one thing only.

> **Marketing is less about selling and more about helping.**

As you begin fine-tuning your marketing strategy, think deeply about how your brand (personal or business) **helps, benefits, and adds value** to other people's lives. It will become much easier to effectively navigate the complexities of marketing. From there, how your brand communicates with the world will shift, and you'll begin to understand what it takes to get people to pause and listen to you, and that's the first step to becoming a CRAVED brand.

Another common misconception about the field of marketing is that (at its core) it's about deception or manipulation. The truth is, it's quite the opposite.

Marketing is not about deception or manipulation at all. Instead, it's about transparency between you and *your* people, showcasing and highlighting all the ways your brand *improves* their lives.

If you're looking to build an influential and inspirational brand, your communication matters. Not only do you need to spark interest and curiosity, but you also need to move people from the 'just-browsing' or 'just scrolling' stage to the lead, prospect, or brand ambassador stage. Effective marketing isn't about closing a sale; it's about creating an experience, and when your experiences are memorable, sales close naturally.

This book is designed to teach you the art of creating a memorable brand experience and help guide you in being more thoughtful, strategic, and ultimately profitable in your brand ventures; whatever they may be. It was developed not only to help clarify low-cost marketing strategies that *really* work but also provide advice and techniques for a wide range of common brand challenges.

Who is this book for?

This book was written to provide digestible tools, insights, and suggestions to:

- Entrepreneurs, Start-Ups, and Small Business Owners
- Bloggers
- Aspiring Influencers
- Content Creators and Creative Directors

How This Book Works

This book was developed as a tool that pinpoints the thoughts and behaviors behind highly-successful brands and entrepreneurial endeavors. It will help you identify areas of improvement as you map out your brand's direction. It is for anyone who has ever wondered what it takes to engage masses, increase profits, and become a respected resource or thought-leader.

This book will not tell you every single detail about marketing because frankly, that's impossible. It's simply too vast a field. Nor will it go into great depth about the dimensions of research and analytics that marketers employ to help shape decision-making. What it will do, however, is provide rationale, direction, and clarity on what it fundamentally takes to become more influential in your industry and continually attract opportunities. It delves into how best to plan, communicate, and execute ideas that will help your brand **stand out**.

You want people to notice you, and you want people to listen to the things you say. That means you *have* to understand the journey of a customer, regardless of whether you're looking to grow a business, blog, or expand your personal brand. You *have* to be different from your competition. You *have* to come across as capable and competent. You *have* to know your audience. You *have* to tell a captivating story. You *have* to have compelling content. You *have* to have a plan. **You *have* to be strategic.**

It is vital that you understand the importance of marketing as a key element of brand sustainability, regardless of your industry or goals. This book will show you how everything is interconnected.

If you're ready to see how marketers build highly successful, CRAVED brands, then let's get started.

PART 1

Get Your Mind Right

CHAPTER 1

The Beliefs and Mindsets Behind Craved Brands

Before you start this journey, it's important that you make sure you've got your mind right. The brand building process is just that—a process; and with any process, you have to pace yourself. Marketing and advertising are not the easiest things to get the hang of. There's no need to try and figure everything out this week, this month, or even this year. Honestly, no one does. All great things take time, so there's no need to try and implement everything you learn right away.

Instead, focus on staying the course despite the uncertainty (because you will face uncertainties). Engross yourself in your goals and make a game-plan that moves you a little closer to those goals daily. Every step matters, even the little ones.

Before you even begin to get your mind right, you have to know one thing—one very vital thing. Behind every successful brand is a person (sometimes a group) with some serious *passion* behind what they do, regardless of what it is. If you desire to make a major personal or professional shift in your life, there needs to be an excitement that lives in you. It's what makes you care and it's what helps you stay focused.

The truth is, passion the **main** ingredient of success. Why? Because passion is what fuels your drive and ambition. Building a brand of any kind requires a great deal of mental energy. In order to keep your mental energy flowing, you'll need to be enthusiastic about your long-term vision, even when you're unable to see how everything will play out. Having passion will help you to be more personally motivated and more fulfilled during the process of becoming this new brand. Whatever goal or lifestyle you're seeking as a result of your endeavors can only be achieved when you commit your mind to be less fearful and more focused.

It's important to know that a brand doesn't just *become* sought-after and CRAVED. Success happens when an idea and a strategy collide and infuse a focused marketing plan to serve as a <u>blueprint</u> for future brand-related decisions.

If you take a look at highly-successful brands, you'll notice one thing they all have in common—they center around solving a problem or filling a specific void. A smart brand will then take that problem and identify the *need* that aligns with it. After the *need* is evident, they determine a myriad of ways to continually address it, becoming a resource, expert, or thought-leader. During that process, great brands then add a whole lot of unique and interesting *content* that is not only sharable and clickable, but likable and showcases them as trustworthy.

SET YOUR INTENTIONS

With a focused plan, anyone, with *any* skillset, in *any* industry, can effectively position themselves as an influential brand and breakthrough ceilings while breaking down barriers.

The goal is brand longevity, and that longevity can only be achieved by understanding the fundamentals of the discipline of marketing so that you can use that knowledge to better communicate and persuade masses of people to listen to and trust you. Building a highly successful, CRAVED brand will take some serious focus. It will require commitment, diligence, consistency, and as a final, friendly reminder—a whole heap of passion.

PASSION MATTERS

Passion is one of those things that's difficult to define. What is passion? I like to think of it as something you really, really care about. It's a feeling and love for something that lives deep in your soul. When you're passionate about something, you're more committed to doing the work that comes along with it. Think bodybuilders. The passion they have for their craft is undeniable. It's what keeps you going when things get tough, and you want to give up. Passion is such a strong emotion that others can feel it in you, and it makes them passionate too. Your conviction and energy around what you do (and why you do it) is contagious. Because people can feel your energy, it's imperative that your energy be both positive and confident. In order for others to believe in you and your brand, you first have to show that you believe in yourself.

Don't Let Your Fears Stop You From Going Full-Speed Ahead

Will having passion alleviate the uneasiness you feel during the brand development process? Unfortunately, no. The uncertainty and anxiety will be there, and those are feelings you'll have to continually train your brain to conquer in order for your brand dreams to become your reality. One of my favorite quotes was spoken by the late Nelson Mandela and reads:

> *"I learned that courage was not the absence of fear, but the triumph over it. The brave man is not he who does not feel afraid, but he who conquers that fear."*

Will you face obstacles?
Certainly.
Successful brands are built by **relentless** individuals that aren't phased by obstacles. Obstacle? What obstacle? A curveball maybe—but not enough of a barrier to stop them from continuing onward.

Will there be naysayers?
Absolutely.
Learn to tune out and distance yourself from negative people. That toxic energy will hinder your creativity and affect your confidence.

Will you have setbacks?
Undoubtedly.

Realize that you will encounter setbacks and challenges during this journey, but they're only temporary. You will recover. Go where you feel most creative and motivated, and start restrategizing. New ideas will emerge.

Will there be change?
Constantly.

Understand that change is a *really* good thing in general (it's where growth happens), and it should be embraced even though you may be unsure of how things will play out long-term. Fears, hurdles, barriers, and change are par for the course any time personal or professional growth is involved. It's important to start looking at change as necessary and beneficial components to improving your life's future outcomes and morphing into who you seek to become.

There's always more creativity inside of you, and sometimes you actually need a little push to unlock it. Difficulties strengthen us because they teach us how to pivot and be more resourceful. There are a ton of ideas in your mind, and ultimately, anything is figureoutable. Focus your energy on being more imaginative and unique, and positive transformations will start to take shape.

Building a successful brand, whether you yourself are the brand, or you're creating a business, will require a lot of you; but at the core, it will require you to persevere despite detours, roadblocks, and closed doors.

It's Time For a Mind Makeover

Getting your mind right often requires a mind-makeover, which can be quite challenging. As someone with a vision, it's appropriate to call you a visionary. Perhaps you're more of a visionary in the making. Either way, you're stepping outside of your comfort zone, and that in itself is worth applauding.

By taking the leap to develop and cultivate a brand or business, you've already made a huge decision that will chart the course of your life, but you must also start reframing your mind to see the possibilities over the difficulties.

It's imperative that you master your mind before you dive into the brand building process because success requires ongoing optimism. You have to think beyond your present situation. Most of the greats had humble beginnings, starting in basements and garages, but they managed to stay optimistic, and most of all, they stayed focused.

> ### *A Worthwhile Read:*
> ### Book Recommendation
>
> "The Four Agreements: A Practical Guide to
> Personal Freedom (A Toltec Wisdom Book),
> by Don Miguel Ruiz.

Get ready, the brand development process is going to be an exhilarating and highly-rewarding ride.

Everything is Challenging at First

Becoming a brand will require some real persistence and diligence. Expect roadblocks along your path. Every idea won't work. Every venture won't pay off. It's important to get a tough shell early and understand that you can rebound from any setback or challenge that comes your way.

Building a successful brand is not for the complacent. A big part of it will require you to get people excited about *what you do* and *why you do it*. In order to get people enthused, you'll likely find yourself repeating yourself over, and over, and over again. You're going to be telling the same story a million times.

Everyone won't be convinced that your brand is worth investing in or listening to, and that's okay—those aren't your people. You have to learn to quickly move on and find others that believe the things you believe. These people do exist. You need to remember your long-term vision and why you started down this path in the first place because there will be times that you think about throwing in the towel.

Another thing worth noting is that you won't always make the right business or brand decisions. You'll lose money, you'll pursue pointless partnerships, and you'll work on projects that don't stick. It's all a part of the process, unfortunately, and it causes a lot of people to give up. Stay the course, learn how to be better at marketing yourself, and ultimately the wins will come. All in all, none of that adversity will matter in the long run and will make for some really great brand stories down the line.

It's true what they say in the gym: no pain, no gain. Learn from the losses so that you know how best to navigate similar situations in the future. Without them, you wouldn't be adequately prepared for this journey.

You may find that your initial business model isn't bringing in enough profit. Okay, in that case, you'll need to restrategize and change it. There's nothing wrong with changing things up whenever you see fit. Perhaps your products aren't selling at the rate you thought they would. Maybe it's that you need new packaging, descriptions, or pricing. Again, everything is challenging at first, and there will be a learning curve.

Don't be deterred or discouraged as you navigate the brand building process. There are things you *have* to learn. There are parts of the process that are supposed to challenge you in order to change and prepare you. As you become more familiar with what matters in marketing, you'll get better at identifying when (and why) you need to make changes to your brand.

Ideas are Only the Beginning

Everyone has great ideas. Everyone. But not everyone with great ideas has a highly successful, CRAVED brand, even if that's their goal. The reason is that they're not willing to do the less-than-pretty things that are needed to advance their vision.

Developing a brand will require some real work (sweat-equity) on your part. It takes more than you proclaiming yourself to be a brand or be in business to have a successful one. You are responsible for getting your brand noticed, which could be anything from writing proposals to giving pitches or attending events. It certainly means developing and sharing content and staying present on social media. Brand building means you have to continually market and seek out opportunities for yourself.

Start by writing down your ideas, then break them out into categories. For each idea, determine the basic steps you need to take to get your thoughts in motion. This isn't the time to sit back and wait. It's a time to think deeply about what you want and start transforming your ideas into achievable and obtainable visions.

DISCIPLINE IS YOUR DIFFERENTIATOR, especially in the early stages of brand and business development. Start by setting priorities for yourself. Create a schedule that outlines your to-dos (and by when). Consider a *monthly* calendar, but get in the habit of updating the individual tasks *weekly*. Be specific in why things need to be done by a given date (even if the real reason only exists in your head). Think of all of the pieces to your brand as a puzzle that you have to put together before you get to your goal.

Drop the Comparisons

You are what you are, and you're not what you're not. It's as simple as that. Most people struggle with what I like to call the "am I worthy" syndrome. We look at other people, and we size them up in comparison to us. Like most people, I too have been guilty of comparing myself to others, and it's stopped me in my tracks more times than I can count.

Knowing what I know now, I wish that I'd had more faith in my previous self, but sometimes it takes a few false starts to really get your engine revved up.

Comparisons steal your joy and make you doubt your individual potential. If someone else can do it, then you *can* do it. If no one else has ever done it, that's all the more reason you *should* do it.

To be successful, you have to tune it all out. You have to make yourself your only competition. You can't focus on what other people are doing; all that matters is what you're doing. Mute the opinions of other people, and your brand's foundation is starting off on the right footing. It's easy to compare yourself because brand competition is everywhere. But, just as competition is everywhere, so are opportunities.

SELF-DOUBT: MY PERSONAL ACCOUNT

Over the course of my life, I tried three separate times to start my own marketing agency. Each time I was super-serious [in my head]. The first two times, the agencies didn't take off because I would look around and think to myself "you could never actually do this." I told myself I was too young or wasn't mentally ready. I'd do frequent searches of leadership pages of top advertising agencies and wouldn't see anyone that looked like me. I got so defeated. It made me constantly question my abilities.

What I was doing was comparing myself to people that ultimately did not matter. Truly there was a void and a lack of representation, but that offered me the opportunity to close the void and add a new look and face to my field. When I stopped looking at what other people were doing, I realized that I was equally as qualified as them (if not more). All I really needed was to have a game plan and a bit of a mindset shift.

We are all guilty of comparing—it's a natural part of life. You have to change your mindset and focus on being your own biggest advocate. Think about what you *want* for you. Ultimately, your brand experience will center largely around your personal strengths and unique qualities. Comparing is a learned behavior, and as such, can be unlearned. You are different from the rest, and that's a good thing. You just have to figure out how best to showcase those differences. Don't worry; we talk in-depth about finding your differentiation and highlighting your uniqueness more in chapter four, "Where You Fit In: Defining Your Brand."

Consistency Above Motivation

You won't always feel like working on your personal brand or entrepreneurial endeavors. That's why you'll need to focus less on being personally motivated, and instead, focus on remaining consistent. Think about it just like working out or eating right. You don't always want to do it, but your weight loss results are tied to your consistency, regardless of how you feel. As you start to fine-tune your brand, your commitment and consistency will make a tremendous difference in your outcomes. Look at your habits first, because consistency starts there. In order to get from where you are now, to where you want to be, you will undoubtedly have to change some of your habits.

Are you willing to get up earlier or stay up until the wee hours of the night to accomplish a task for your brand? That's what it's going to take sometimes. New York Times best-selling author and psychologist Angela Duckworth describes this as "grit." In her book of the same name, she talks about how success is less about talent and genius and more about a deep determination for a specific outcome. The root of that determination is continued consistency. Ultimately, this consistency will be what sets your brand up to flourish.

QUICK TIP: START BY SELF-REFLECTING

Identify two to three habits that you think will hold you back. Examples might be that you procrastinate or make excuses for why things don't get done. It then becomes a matter of willpower and focusing on becoming more consistent. You have to be willing to be temporarily uncomfortable because you know that in the long-run, you desire a much different lifestyle.

When I first entered into entrepreneurship, I had no idea what I was in for. All of sudden I was able to create my own destiny and set my own rules. I thought that my days of having a routine were out the window, but I couldn't have been more wrong. Having a routine is just as important for personal endeavors as it is for someone working a 9-5. Having a routine doesn't mean that every day works the exact same, it just means that you infuse some type of structure into your days to help you stay focused and on track. I've found that planning my week's to-dos in advance helps me keep my priorities straight and procrastinate less.

At the start of the week, I write down my tasks and identify what I like to call my "non-negotiables" for the day. Those are the things that I must accomplish by the day's end. I had to start acting as my own drill sergeant and so will you. There will be times you have to force yourself to complete certain tasks, remembering that ultimately your brand success is up to you.

Don't Let Past Failures Define You

Odell Beckham Jr., a wide receiver in the National Football League, once said this:

> *"Life stuff happens. You get knocked down, and you get back up. That's just always been my mentality. I'm not really fazed by anything. It's in the past. There's nothing I can really do about it now. You learn from it, and you move on."*

It's time to reframe how you think about *failure* because the truth is, you don't really fail, and you don't really lose—you learn. You learn how to do things differently in the future and you gain knowledge that you wouldn't otherwise have had if things worked out differently.

When things don't go as planned, it's a catalyst for you to change direction and be more intentional about the next move you make.

My mentality about failure is aligned with that of actor Will Smith. He took to Instagram late in 2018 to talk about how important and beneficial it is to fail at things. He made what has since become a series of viral videos where he said, *"It's always a little bit frustrating to me when people have a negative relationship with failure...Failure is a massive part of being able to be successful. You have to get comfortable with failure. You have to actually seek failure. Failure is where all the lessons are."*

So, to piggyback on that, I encourage you not to get hung up on things of the past that didn't work out. They were supposed to happen the way they did. They should not, however, deter you from continuing on your path. In case you need a friendly reminder, this dream (your dream) is worth fighting for.

More than that, I believe that our failures are not accidental, but are tied to our purpose. There was something you needed to learn, and there is a story you need to be able to tell.

Learn to take the lessons from the past and continue pushing forward. Know that a setback is never the end of the road. In fact, I think failing gives you wings. It presents a new opportunity for you to fly in a different direction. Dust yourself off, and plan to make your next move your best move.

FROM A SETBACK TO A COMEBACK

Each setback allows you the chance to think bigger than you ever have before. Plus, your future million-dollar brand doesn't have time to be consumed with things of the past.

The good thing is, telling your stories of failure (and triumph over them) can position your brand for monumental impact and opportunity. In fact, it's actually marketing gold. People don't identify with perfection because it's not real. Nor is it relatable.

When you're ready to share how you prevailed and triumphed from all the things that tried to break you, the public will be ready to listen and support you.

You're so badass, and you don't even know it. Now that you know the mindset you'll need to embody in order to successfully embark on building your brand, let's get into the nitty-gritty, shall we?

IS IT ME, OR IS THE WORD 'MARKETING' EVERYWHERE?

You hear it all the time, but chances are, no one has ever taken the time to clearly explain what marketing actually is, or what it *truly* entails. All you probably know is that, whatever marketing is, you need to do it well if you're looking to build a personal brand or game-changing business venture.

Most people think of marketing as commercials, magazine ads, radio spots, billboards, websites, logos, tradeshows, flyers, signage, and so on. To most non-marketers, this field seems like a fun, creative, flashy business that focuses more on being cute and catchy and less on data, planning, analysis, and measurement. In actuality, however, although marketing is one of the more artistic parts of business, marketers very much mean business. Marketing is all of the above, and so, so much more.

THE WHAT
MARKETING, DEMYSTIFIED

What is marketing, really?

Honestly, a more appropriate place to start is with what marketing **is not**.

Marketing is *not* promotion. Marketing is *not* selling. Marketing is *not* media. Marketing is *not* signage. Marketing is *not* ads. Marketing is *not* brochures.

<u>Marketing, unfortunately, is not just...one thing.</u>

In its simplest form, **marketing is the <u>process</u> of getting people to care about what you do and why you do it.** It's connecting with people in a way that makes them pause for a moment, and hopefully a lifetime, because not only were they impressed by you, they loved you. So, as they move through life, those people remember you. They advocate for you. They tell others about you. They become loyal to you. They believe in and trust you. That's marketing—simplified.

Sure promotion, media, and creative pieces like brochures and flyers compliment the process, but by themselves, they certainly don't represent all that this field includes.

Does that mean that marketing is easy? Certainly not. However, good marketing is at the root of opportunities, sales, and profit, both for personal brands and business ventures. It's how you see continuous growth and longevity. Marketing is what transforms a brand from an option to a priority.

So then, what is a brand?

A brand is *not* a logo. A brand is *not* a website. A brand is *not* a trademark, patent, or copyright. A brand is *not* a product or service.

A brand is an experience.
It's a promise and a commitment to people.

A brand can be challenging to explain because every brand means and represents something different to people depending on who you ask. I like to think of a brand as a series of meaningful moments, experiences, and interactions.

That may feel like an ambiguous answer, but how people experience you is really what defines who *you* are as a brand. A brand can be a person or a business. In fact, these days more and more people are developing dynamic personal brands that make them respected and highly influential.

The correct series of meaningful moments can lead to an uber-powerful, game-changing, massively profitable brand.

Successful brands, both personal and business, have dynamic, focused marketing plans that include clear goals and sound strategies. They seek to continually evolve because staying the same doesn't bring progression. They take risks, they're creative, they're professional, and they're innovative. They stand for something, and that stance does not waver. They make good on their word and focus on their impact on others over themselves. They believe in what they do and that belief makes others believe too.

Wrapping Things Up

Marketing and branding are very different components, but they work together as partners. One doesn't effectively exist without the other. Now is a good time to start thinking about the **experience** of *you* as a brand.

» How do you *want* to make people feel, and how will you go about that?

» How do you *want* people to interact with you?

» Why should people *trust* you?

» What do you *want* people to know about you?

Brand clarity isn't something to take lightly. Your brand livelihood depends largely on how people experience you. **Get comfortable being uncomfortable** because that's part of this journey. Know that the results of the work you're doing now will not be instantaneous, but they will come in time. Be patient but persistent. Realize that you'll have to make some short-term sacrifices for long-term rewards. It's time to start being more intentional about all the things you want your brand to embody.

CHAPTER 2

Today's Consumer Mindset

Humans need things to survive. Thinking only about the basics for a minute, humans need food, shelter, and clothing. Everything else is technically a perk. That includes your new car with heated seats and a backup camera, the 50-inch TV that's mounted on the wall in your living room, the organic strawberries sitting on your kitchen counter, the artwork that hangs in your hallway, the hand-painted mug you drink your tea in, and the watch that you wear on your wrist.

Yes, it's true that humans *need* things; but it's also true that humans *want* things. Every one of us is a consumer of something. Think about it like this. Consuming is driving past four brick-oven pizza restaurants because you love that Sal's Pizzeria has more cheese options, always cooks your crust to the perfect crisp, and lets you get shrimp as a topping. Consuming is also you, walking past 15 personal trainers in the gym until you get to the one you're confident will help you drop the 10 pounds you gained during the Thanksgiving holiday.

Consuming is the flight you book to go to Vegas for a long weekend, and the airline you take to get you there. It's your decision to take Lyft to the Marriott instead of a taxi. It's the shows you see and the stores you buy from while you're there. Consuming is the music you listen to, the television shows you watch, the social media pages you follow, the clothes you buy, and the car you drive. Consuming is *every* decision you make.

We all consume. You, me, your best friend, your mom, your dad, your partner, your children; everyone. Humans consume not only to survive but also to live more comfortably and happily. Yes, you may need a pair of sneakers because you're doing your first half-marathon and want your feet to be comfortable. However, your decision to purchase Nike over New Balance is a personal choice. That choice affords you an opportunity to try and stand out enough to be the brand that's chosen.

To say that people have choices is a vast understatement. We have lots of choices. Lots, and lots, and lots of choices. We have more choices and options than we've ever had before, and this variety and competition is why brands have to work harder than ever to be unique, in order to command a place in the market.

All day, every day we're bombarded with people trying to get our attention.

» "Hey, check out these great travel deals that I can offer you. I can get you and a friend to Dubai for $798 round-trip. Everything's included— flight, hotel, meals, and transfer. This is the travel package for you."

» "This laptop is better because it gives you 16GB of RAM, has a 1TB hard drive, and has a larger screen, which will help you be a better graphic designer. This is the best laptop for your needs."

» "This comforter set is made from down feathers, which means you'll sleep more peacefully, and you'll be more rested. This is the comforter of all comforters. "

» "Got acne-prone skin? This product is 70% salicylic acid and gets so deep in your pores your acne will disappear in 14 days. This is the face wash you need."

» "Our purses are 100% vegan leather, so no animals were killed in making this bag. Plus, they are super-chic and go with your busy lifestyle. This is the purse you need."

» "Our online certificate program will help put you in more demand as you grow in your career. Plus, our program is only six weeks so you won't have to invest a lot of time, but the long-term payoff will be huge. This is the educational program you need."

» "Need small business advice? We have over 25 years supporting small business and helping them launch great ideas. We're the consultants you need."

» "Looking to meet new people or find local events in your area? Our event site updates in real-time and shows you events tailored to your interests. Download our app."

EVERYBODY'S GOT A PROMISE.

On any given day, we see or hear hundreds of different promos on everything from teeth whitening to self-help. Between radio and television, social media and email, we're bombarded with people trying to convince us to choose them, or follow them, or purchase their services. It's exhausting. We honestly feel like we know how to find the things we need and want. I like to call this mentality "leave me alone, I'll be in touch if and when I need something from you."

The Consumer of Today is Inundated

People are busy, tired, overwhelmed, and exhausted. They're juggling demanding jobs, family, friendships, and personal struggles. They're trying to get or stay healthy, manage stress and mental health, stay on top of their responsibilities, spend time with loved ones, and enjoy the little pleasures of life as best they can. Additionally, people are trying to save money.

But, consumers still consume and will continue consuming the things that they find **value** in. For those looking to build a successful brand, it's imperative that you have a *deep* understanding of the people you want to be in front of.

All day, every day, someone is trying to get money from us. If not money, then time. If not money or time, then commitment. Often, it's all three.

Today's consumers are keenly aware that all three are incredibly valuable, and so they are very guarded. Plus, nowadays, life is on-demand. Practically everything we want is available at the touch of a button. At any time, for any reason, we can pick up our phones and get answers to questions, find solutions to our challenges, and buy exactly what we're looking for.

Before we take a deep dive into who today's consumers are, let's go back in time for just a minute. It's important to remember how life, as we know it, has evolved (and how society has shifted vastly) in recent years before you can fully understand what it takes to build powerful brand connections in present-day.

Do you recall the year 2000? It seems like eons ago, but in a relatively short number of years, the world has undergone some of the most rapid technological transformations we've ever seen. With new technology entering our lives weekly, consumers have started to demand even more from the brands they support. Technology, connectivity and reachability are now at the core of influence. How people connect with you and find you matters. It's a huge part of your brand experience and should not be overlooked.

In 2000, our primary methods of communication outside of our homes were pagers and clunky portable phones. Mobile apps, no way. Computers were bulky and slow; and compared to the ultra-sleek, elaborate models of today, super-limited in their capabilities. Faxing was how we quickly distributed information, which has now been replaced by email, text, and social media. CDs were once the go-to for video and music, but now we rely on streaming. Technology has changed everything.

With every new technological change, consumers have become more and more in control of how brands adapt to meet their needs and expectations. That includes *your* brand.

Need a new coffee maker? There's no need to get in the car and drive 20 minutes to the store and search aisle by aisle. Now, all you have to do is go to Google or Bing, enter some quick details, and you'll have it in hand in less than seven days (or in two, if you have Amazon Prime). Plus, on any given day, people can use smart speakers with voice-recognition to do or find just about anything.

PEOPLE ARE EMPOWERED

This ease of information and access to the world has created a really impatient and really empowered consumer. Anytime you think you're the only one struggling with patience, just sit at a light 0.06 seconds after it turns green. The immediate surge of horn-honks will show you just how impatient people these days are.

Every time I'm at Starbucks standing in the line to order, I watch hordes of people walk past the line, grab the drinks they pre-ordered online, and dash out the door. Our expectations are much different than they used to be.

Nowadays we search for products based on shipping times, we leave websites that don't load fast enough, and we love when a company remembers our information so that we don't have to reenter it every time we're ready to buy. In order to establish a brand or business that thrives in this type of environment, you have to understand who you're dealing with.

WHAT YOU NEED TO KNOW ABOUT TODAY'S CONSUMERS

They're impatient. They're informed. They're connected. Always. They're self-aware. They're easily turned off.

To marketers, understanding people's behavior is our lifeblood. In order to effectively connect with people, we conduct in-depth analyses that help guide every component of marketing from strategy (direction), to timing (predictions), to messaging (framing), to channel (distribution). Understanding the modern consumer's mind will help your brand speak the right language and determine the best ways to get the right people listening to you.

Your goal is to stand out and make consumers choose you.

Because we're inundated nonstop, we've learned to tune out most promotions. That means you can't afford not to know what today's consumers expect. It will be instrumental in shaping your influence and in helping you outshine your competition.

THE MODERN-DAY MENTALITY

WHAT DO WE WANT?

EVERYTHING.

WHEN DO WE WANT IT?

YESTERDAY.

HOW DO WE WANT TO GET IT?

WITH THE LEAST HASSLE POSSIBLE.

Impatient.

Life today is on-demand. The things we're looking for, we can find—and we can find quickly. With phone in hand, we're scrolling through websites and apps ordering everything from groceries to sweaters to coffee, or boots, or flowers, maybe a car, or possibly even a home. Practically nothing is off limits these days.

Life is so convenient from our phones and computers that convenience is now ingrained in our expectations. That means that if a brand is considered inconvenient, people get aggravated and move to one that presents less of a hassle for them. People are multitasking like crazy, so they like things to be easy. They have to get back to juggling all the other components of their busy lives.

As the world continues moving faster and faster, people have become more impatient. Honestly, these days, you don't have to have much (if any) human interaction to get most things done. So, overall as a society, we've come to expect to get the things we want quickly. This is important to keep in mind as you carve out your brand advantage and is especially true for entrepreneurs looking to capitalize on a business brand.

Informed.

The consumer of today knows a lot, definitely more than those of the past. Thank Google, Bing, and Yahoo! for that. Searching online is now so much a part of daily life that there are over **3.5 billion online searches performed every day**. If there's one thing people know how to do well, it's find answers online.

We ask the internet questions, and we expect correct and helpful responses. We explore ideas on our own, and seek out solutions often without speaking to, or engaging with, another human in the process.

We feel like we can do more on our own than ever. Because we're searching online, the first rule of thumb is that your brand be findable on the internet. It's imperative that consumers are able to locate your brand online. First and foremost, you need to have a digital presence and show up in search engines. Society equates credibility with online findability; so to be trusted and respected, you must establish yourself online first.

Always Connected.

To say we're a connected society really is an understatement. We're online and on our phones all day checking everything from emails to weather conditions. We're watching videos, reading news, conducting business, skimming social media apps, shopping, dating, and listening to music (just to name a few). We're obsessed with data and Wi-Fi, and we want to be able to get online whenever we desire to be entertained and educated.

All of this multitasking and connectivity may make you feel like it's easier to reach people, but in actuality, that's not always the case. In all that we're doing on our computers and phones, we start ignoring the things that are right in front of our faces.

The more promotions we see, the more we miss. Advertisements become a part of our norm, just something else to ignore.

A study by Microsoft identified that the average consumer's attention span is only eight seconds. Think about that. Eight seconds is often all you get. How will your brand say the right things to make the eight-second cut? Is what you're saying memorable enough in eight seconds to get consumers to pause, listen, and remember you? Or, are you just another brand to scroll past and ignore? Brands need to be properly positioned for success. In part three of this book, we walk through the best ways to position your brand to make the eight-second cut.

Self-Aware.

Today's consumers know themselves—well. They know what they like, but more so, they know what they don't like. One of the most important elements to be mindful of when talking to today's consumer is that they are highly self-aware. They take the initiative to explore and learn about things on their own.

Being self-aware is closely tied to being informed but is separated out because there are a few slight differences. Someone could just watch tons of news, and thus they consider themselves educated on certain subjects. Self-awareness, however, links closely to skepticism. The truth is, people are skeptical. Very skeptical. Marketers call this the "age of information." Consumers are basically saying "okay, I hear you, but before I really trust you, let me do my own research." The fact is, people initially trust their own answers more than yours.

How many times have you been sick and gone online to see if you could identify what was wrong with you? Your friend told you it was probably just a cold, but you went on WebMD, typed in your symptoms—and all of a sudden, you're dying. Ha! People are self-aware but also dramatic. Understanding that consumers critically consume information will help you as you identify the tools your brand will need to differentiate itself to a society that prides itself on being self-aware and self-taught.

Easily Turned Off.

These days it doesn't take much for people to throw their hands up and walk away from a brand, personal or business. People have high expectations and won't tolerate poor customer service, broken promises, sneaky business practices, or insensitivity.

Consumers today demand stellar brand experiences; otherwise, you can expect frustration to be shared with anyone who will listen, including social media. It's vital that you spend time listening. People have lots to say, and it can be incredibly helpful to hear them out as you start to strategize and plan your brand takeover.

In addition to living in the "age of information," we're also living in the "age of convenience," and in our highly technological world, you can do almost anything in a matter of seconds. There are an abundance of options and alternatives readily available, so why should we give *you* a second chance? In order to make sure your brand isn't a turn-off, focus on being inclusive, knowledgeable, relatable, reliable, and unique (oh, and don't be too uptight, it tends to turn consumers off).

TODAY'S WORLD MOVES AT RAPID SPEEDS

How people decide *what* to buy has changed. Consumers are not as loyal as they once were to big, well-known brands. Today, it's about who can provide us the things we're looking for in the most convenient, quick, and personalized way possible.

Enter entrepreneurs, bloggers, influencers, and small businesses. That leaves real opportunity for you to come in and disrupt the marketplace, and disruption is good. Actually, disruption is great. Brand disruption means you've come with something innovative and different than what people are used to.

MEETING CONSUMER NEEDS & WANTS

Evaluate your brand in relation to today's consumer mindset. How can your brand be convenient? Perhaps it's that consumers will be able to purchase your products and services online.

How can your brand inform consumers of your expertise? Is it through blog posts, articles, videos, or something else? These are discussed in later chapters in this book but start thinking about them now. How will you ensure your brand doesn't turn people off? Remember, experiences matter. Start to think about the experience you want to create.

Of course, these characteristics are general assumptions and certainly not applicable to every audience, especially as you start dissecting different populations like Baby Boomers vs. Generation X vs. Millennials vs. Generation Z.

It's good practice to get in the habit of digging around the internet and library before making any big brand-related changes. It's important (and incredibly helpful) to know what's already out in the market, who's dominating your space, and how your target consumers are responding to it. A traditionalist will be looking for very different things than a millennial, so understanding your people and your industry will provide really good intel that ultimately enables you to make smarter decisions for your brand. To marketers, these types of research and audits are essential parts of our field. We dig around for months (sometimes even years) before deciding the best courses of action. Marketing is much more than just catchy advertisements. There are so many things being considered behind the scenes.

One thing that's always a factor to consumers is convenience. Since it matters to consumers, it matters to marketers. Convenience means you're making it easy for people to reach you, engage with you, work with you, and ultimately buy from you.

DON'T INCONVENIENCE PEOPLE

Regardless of what type of brand you're developing, keep the idea of convenience top-of-mind. Convenience can be anything from location or proximity to *your* people, to being able to purchase your products and services online. Being seen as an inconvenience will limit your brand's growth.

CONSUMERS ARE SKEPTICAL

Regardless of what you do or sell, your job as a brand is to get people to notice and listen to you. Because modern-day life allows us to find so much of the information we need on our own, we've become inherently doubtful of people that appear out of nowhere claiming that they have the golden eggs to problem-solving. So, instead, we just don't listen, or we half-listen, and then we move on. As consumers are more self-aware, they are also becoming their own best problem-solvers.

People know what they're looking for. They may not know where they're going to get it, but they generally know what they'd like the outcome to be. This is actually a huge benefit to your brand because that makes it easier to determine what to say to get people listening to you.

Before anyone believes that you are an expert at something, you have to persuade people through your credibility. Experience and credibility go hand in hand. Consumer skepticism, combined with an abundance of options, means that people want to know, down to the detail, what makes you an **expert** on a given topic.

QUICK TIP: LET PEOPLE KNOW HOW YOU THINK

People aren't mind readers, so the best way to get someone to buy into your brand is to share your thoughts, expertise, and beliefs on various subjects and topics.

BUILDING YOUR CREDIBILITY
Where to Start

Create Resources

Credibility often starts with content. Content, in its simplest form, means creating and distributing resources that relate to your expertise. The goal is for the content to paint you as knowledgeable (and likable), thus attracting people to you. The goal of content is to position you as an expert or influential figure, so you need to be intentional in everything you attach to your brand, and ultimately to your name. We talk more about content marketing in chapter seven, "Craft Your Content Like a Boss," but for now, think about the various ways you can best showcase your expertise. Perhaps you can start by writing short articles or blog posts on topics that interest the people you'd like to notice you. Maybe you think a video is a better way to showcase your capabilities. Or, perhaps it would be worthwhile to do both. It's up to you. Both are effective.

If you're thinking about video as your currency for credibility, don't worry, we dive into all things video marketing in chapter nine, "Using Video to Revolutionize Your Brand." Mixing up how you showcase your expertise is good because everyone learns and digests information differently.

The things that capture person A's attention might not catch person B's—and you want them both to crave your brand, which means your content needs to be strategic.

Expand Your Network

Brand building and strong relationships go hand in hand. Relationships are fundamental for long-term and continuous brand growth. Find local events that center around your brand's focus or ideal consumer. Find a mentor that's been where you've been and can walk you through the unknowns. As you build your network and meet new people, it's important to remember that you're still responsible for pushing your brand agenda forward. Always conduct yourself with professionalism and be a shining example of what brand excellence and real commitment looks like.

Volunteer or Do Freebies

Everyone wants to come out of the gate making money for their expertise, but it often doesn't work like that. Volunteering or providing your knowledge for free is a great way to start to grow your connections and name in your industry. It's also a good way to build a portfolio of work and gain more experience.

Find a few people or causes that align with your brand goals and get in touch with them. Offer your products, services, or expertise at no charge. Not only will this help you build your portfolio, volunteering and helping others is good for the soul. Be sure that the work you do is dynamic because the people you're working with will remember you. Because you want this experience to set the stage for your brand success and longevity, be sure to do stellar work from start to finish, even if the return isn't monetary.

AN INSIDE PERSPECTIVE
HOW NETWORKING CHANGED MY LIFE

When I first entered into entrepreneurship, everyone told me to focus on relationship building and networking. Admittedly though, I wasn't a big fan of it, primarily because the idea of chatting with strangers gave me anxiety.

One regular Tuesday afternoon in the summer, I was website-hopping and came across a free seminar on how to do business with the government. It was the same seminar I'd planned to attend six months earlier but never made it. This time though, I gave myself a pep talk and dragged myself to the seminar with limited expectations and no real goals.

That seminar was the catalyst to changing

how I looked at networking. I met five people at the seminar that would go on to land me 17 new clients within the next three months. Just by talking, sharing my expertise, and listening to their challenges and needs, the offers began flooding my inbox. After that, you couldn't tell me not to go to an event that might offer me new business relationships. It opens up so many doors. You never know who knows who.

Create a Portfolio of Your Work

If you have a brand, you should have a place that directs people to learn more about it. It's likely that place will be a website (or even a social media page). Your website and social pages can serve a number of purposes beyond just telling people what you do.

Because industries are more competitive than ever, having an online portfolio is one of the best ways to showcase what you're capable of. People want to check you out before they commit to anything. This is your opportunity to show off your expertise, skills, past work experience, accomplishments, and strengths.

Get a Polished Bio

Although a bio only provides a quick snapshot of your life and accomplishments, when a bio is good, people immediately want to learn more about you and your brand. A strong bio can open up a world of possibilities and make you unforgettable.

Your bio is self-presentation at its best. Improve your chances of being CRAVED out of the gate by making people like you, but even more so, trust you by developing a lively and informative bio that shares some of your experiences and expertise.

Start Collecting Testimonials

Testimonials make people feel safe. How many times do you read the reviews of something before deciding to buy or partner with someone? Consumers are skeptical, remember? And that's okay. Knowing that people battle with skepticism makes it easier for you to be intentional about developing content that persuades them.

Strong testimonials make people curious to want to know more. They demonstrate how your expertise is helpful to other people. Since consumers are looking for answers to their questions, good testimonials explain why you're the best person to provide those answers. To ensure you get high-quality testimonials, make sure you consistently do high-quality work.

Wrapping Things Up

People expect a lot, but there's room for underdogs to disrupt industries by continually meeting consumer expectations and by filling a void.

Don't wait for opportunities, create them. You'll need to get comfortable with promoting yourself, as you are your biggest brand asset. Check out chapter 11, "Brand Yourself for Demand," for more insight on how to stand out and showcase your uniqueness.

CHAPTER 3

The Customer is the Boss

Jeff Bezos, founder and CEO of Amazon, can be famously quoted as saying: **"Your brand is what other people say about you when you're not in the room."**

Think about that for a moment. What might people say about your brand when you're not in the room to hear it? Would they likely say things like you're helpful, trustworthy, communicative, and knowledgeable; or would they instead be more inclined to say things like you're unresponsive, unprofessional, unethical, or hard to get a hold of? Would they say your brand is experienced or amateur, empathetic or indifferent, clear or vague, or accessible or unapproachable? Every perception shapes how people interact with you.

A big part of marketing lies in how people experience you and how you make people feel. That's what they'll remember most about you. Often times the quality of your product matters substantially less than the experience someone had actually interacting with you. **People remember experiences**. So, failing to meet your expectations or not providing good experiences can affect your brand's footing before you even start solidifying yourself within your market.

IMPRESSIONS & PERCEPTIONS MATTER

The minute your conversation is over and you either leave the room or get off the phone, your [potential] customer talks about you. They judge you. They judge every single thing you said, and they size you up. You want to be sure that the impressions you're leaving are favorable or else you likely won't see the success you hope for.

Instead of jumping right into what customers are *really* looking for, I first want to share three of the most common mistakes [I see] from individuals looking to develop a personal brand or business. These blunders impact your brand before you're even out the gate, so it's important that you pause and think through your brand's audience, identity, and experience at inception.

1. Make sure you have a website.

The number one question I get at the brand planning stage is "do I need a website?" I always immediately answer, yes. A brand (of any kind) *definitely* needs a website. Why? Because people don't know you and more so, they don't trust you. A website is typically not the only piece of the pie you'll need in your pool of persuasion, but it's certainly a main ingredient. Regardless of what you do, who you are, where you're trying to go, and who you ultimately want to be—yes, you need a website.

Anyone looking to build themselves as a personal brand, whether it's a coach, consultant, blogger, or influencer, needs a personal brand website. Entrepreneurs who own (or plan to own) a business should have a website for that business.

Why is a website a requirement? Think back to the previous chapter where we talked about how skeptical people are. Having a website is the quickest way to paint yourself as credible. It doesn't need to be a huge undertaking, in fact, the best websites are clean and straightforward. Busy websites with too much text or clutter turn people off. Just think about your site as your chance for show and tell. If you have photos and videos, share them here. People don't just want to know *what* you do, they want to know *who* you are. Have fun and make sure that all of your pages load properly and contain up-to-date information on you, your expertise, your products, and your services.

Lastly, use your website to showcase success stories from people you've worked with. Think of it as your house, *your online home.* This is your opportunity to walk people from room-to-room pointing out all the wonderful and amazing ways that you improve people's lives. Although it's about you, it's really about them. What are they missing if they don't work with you?

2. Do a great deal of research.

Research matters, because in the long run, it will save you time and money. Who wants to make costly marketing mistakes? No one. Spend time researching your industry, including trends and changes. Some industries move faster than others. If you're in a rapidly changing industry, you may need to do monthly or quarterly research to ensure that what you're doing is still relevant. Research doesn't have to be scary.

Search engines are your friend. Doing some quick searches of successful brands will give you a significant advantage over your competition. How to research and what to look for is discussed in chapter five, "What's Brand Growth Without a Strategy."

3. Plan and strategize.

It's important that you have a solid game plan and strategy if you *really* want to make your mark. You need a roadmap and clear goals to help you predict your moves and realistically plan for both growth and roadblocks. Details on goal setting and planning are also discussed in chapter five, "What's Brand Growth Without a Strategy."

QUICK TIP: YOU DON'T WANT TO BE THE CONFUSING BRAND

Instead, you want to be the reputable, easy-to-find, easy-to-contact, cohesive brand. You want to be the brand that people remember and trust. You want to be the brand that people tell other people to check out. Your website, the industry research you take the time to conduct, and your strategic roadmap will help position your brand for standout success.

THE CUSTOMER'S EXPECTATION OF SATISFACTION

We live in a world of options, options, options, and oh yes, more options. Not much is really unique or original anymore. There's always an alternative product or business, and consumers know that. Yes, they may favor one brand over another, but what's more important to them is how something makes them feel. People look to brands to satisfy a feeling or need, and something as simple as making someone smile can lead to big returns.

Start thinking about the feelings or needs that you want your brand to satisfy for people. How do you want to make people feel?

WHAT NEED DOES YOUR BRAND FILL?

The key to consumer satisfaction is fulfilling some type of **need** for a set group of people. All consumers really want are their problems solved, whatever those problems may be. Those problems are vast and open up the door for anyone with a creative mind and a sound marketing plan to come in and change the game.

SIMPLER, BETTER, OR EASIER

BRAND SATISFACTION, DEMYSTIFIED

» A chef who does meal-prep makes people's lives easier and simpler because they help decrease (or eliminate) the time and work that goes into preparing a meal.

» A babysitter or nanny makes people's life better because they help free up time for parents to get more things accomplished.

» A grocery store mobile app makes people's lives easier, better, and simpler because it allows people to order food and household items from anywhere and get them delivered to their door whenever they want.

» A kid's face-painting company makes people's lives better because they put a smile on children's faces and make events more memorable.

» A top-quality knife set makes people's lives better and easier because the ultra-sharp blades mean consumers spend less time prepping food and more time actually enjoying meals and company.

» A travel group makes people's lives <u>better</u>, <u>easier</u>, and <u>simpler</u> because people no longer have to do the logistical trip planning and organizing, and they can just pack and show up at the airport ready to go.

» An eczema skin cream makes people's lives <u>better</u> because now that person's skin is not red, itchy, or inflamed, and they are more confident.

WHAT PROBLEM DOES YOUR BRAND SOLVE?

Before you can think about becoming successful in your brand endeavors, you have to be able to **articulate** the problem that your brand solves. Beyond that, you need to know how to connect the dots and convey to people that you are the one they should choose to solve that problem. The best way is through a strong brand story. See chapter six, "Connect and Captivate With Your Brand Story."

As unfortunate as it sounds, in truth, people don't really care about what you sell. More so, they likely aren't eager to buy what you sell. What really matters to people is themselves. So, in order to increase the likelihood of people listening to you, don't self-promote. Consumers, social media followers, and business investors alike don't appreciate smugness. You will come across as self-absorbed and arrogant, and consumers will be much less inclined to interact with you.

Think about your favorite restaurant. You see pictures of appetizers and entrees that make your mouth water. You can't wait to get back to that restaurant. For consumers, not only do we get access to their delicious meal options, we also get an all-around great experience that makes us feel good. Even though they're showing you how tasty their food is, the end goal is to showcase how much you'll enjoy eating their food.

ENTER: WHAT'S IN IT FOR ME

THE 'WHAT'S IN IT FOR ME' MENTALITY

Affectionately known by marketers as WIIFM, the *what's in it for me? mentality* is the question that nearly every consumer thinks about before deciding to move forward in engaging with a brand or business.

WHAT DO PEOPLE REALLY WANT TO KNOW ABOUT YOU?

People want to know [unequivocally] how your brand will make their lives easier, better, or simpler.

Are you focused on what your customer is focused on? Because your customer is focused on themselves.

» Will this make me look skinnier? [Okay, I want it.]

» Are you sure this will mask my bald spots? [Okay, I want it.]

» Will this trip package get me and my wife to Bali for under $2,000? [Okay, I want it.]

» Will this accent chair make my living room look chicer and still be comfortable to sit in? [Okay, I want it.]

» Will these trash bags hold all of my family's garbage without the tie breaking? [Okay, I want them.]

» Will earning this degree get me a better job or a raise? [Okay, sign me up.]

» Does this phone take good pictures at night? [Okay, I'll take it.]

» Will getting that cosmetic laser treatment remove the dark spots under my eyes? [Okay, I want it.]

» Will having you as my nutritionist help me reverse my pre-diabetes? [Okay, let's get to work.]

» Will these light bulbs last longer and save me money long-term? [Okay, I want them.]

» Will this course teach me how to sell my photography online? [Okay, sign me up.]

» Will having you as my life coach get me out of this 5-year rut I've been in? [Okay, I want to book my sessions.]

Consumers are focused on their own interests, and in order for your brand to be successful, you need to be just as focused on them as they are. One of the most common marketing mistakes brands make is focusing on themselves (and what they want), as opposed to focusing on the things the consumer cares about.

In my fourth year of consulting, I started working with an entrepreneur named Harris Broward. He owned a skincare line and was making over 20 different products. He had hand creams, shower gels, moisturizing lotions, and foot creams. He'd been trying to sell his products for nearly 18 months, but sales were low month-after-month. He'd been losing money developing products that weren't being purchased. Plus, since the ingredients he used were organic, the lifespan of his products was shorter than many of his competitors, which meant they needed to be sold or risk expiring.

During our initial meetings, Harris ran down all of the useful properties in his products and told me the ins-and-out of why organic ingredients were so important in skin care. When I went to his website, I saw that he used 90% of his web platform to talk about how he created his products and walk people through the development process. Though his passion was evident, his profits were consistently low. I realized early on that the missing ingredient in his formula was that he hadn't thought or incorporated the principles of

WIIFM. So, during our second meeting, we spent two hours going product-by-product to identify what mattered most to *consumers*. <u>I wanted him to think past the process of creating each item and instead focus on the results and the outcomes</u>. What mattered more than how these were developed was what people actually got as a result of using them. The first thing I had Harris do was draft some language that he would use in a promotional email.

Here's what he came up with:

"Greetings! We offer a variety of hand creams, shower gels, lotions, and foot creams to help you stay moisturized this winter. Explore our selection and stock up as the weather changes."

I read it and thought, sure, you're telling people *what* you have. It even suggests that the [potential] customer order before the temperature drops. What this doesn't do, however, is tell people *why* they need it. It doesn't tell me *why* I would want to stop what I'm doing to go browse through your products. It certainly doesn't convince me to buy anything.

Harris and I spent the next few hours living and breathing WIIFM. In the end, he asked that I take the lead on revising the language so that he could get a feel for how to think about this moving forward.

The new language [using WIIFM] read:

"Our bodies have 25-40 layers of skin, and that skin needs to be hydrated and cared for to avoid drying, oil build-ups, breakouts, and discoloration. Our vitamin-infused hand creams, face masks, lotions, and foot creams will help keep your skin clear as the chilly air wreaks havoc on your body's natural hydration. This winter, prevent dryness by stocking up on our organic products, and keep your skin moisturized, blemish-free, and younger looking."

The email promotion then went on to highlight the key benefits of four select products before directing people to his website to purchase.

In the first email send, Harris had only sold three products, and those were to long-time, repeat customers. He'd made $72 in revenue from his original email but had hoped it would be a huge profit generator for his brand. In the second email send, however, where we flipped the messaging to focus on what the consumer wants, Harris ended up selling 188 products and made over $4,500 in revenue. That one email brought in more profit than he'd seen the entire time he'd been in business. Although the WIIFM version ended up being longer in length, it was more explanatory (and educational), tied the product to the consumer problem, and highlighted a variety of benefits to appeal to the most people possible.

More Explanatory	· Original text: 31 words · WIIFM text: 76 words
Identified the Consumer Problem	· Avoid drying, oil build ups, breakouts, and discoloration · You have dryer skin in the winter months, which calls for more intentional skincare routines to keep you properly hydrated
Highlighted a Variety of Benefits	· Keeps your skin moisturized · Blemish-free · Younger looking

In addition to expecting to be told *how* they'll benefit, people also want to <u>trust</u> the brand they're using before moving into the commitment stage. That trust starts with you showing the consumer you know what you're talking about. By adding in details about the layers of skin our bodies have, Harris' credibility sky-rocketed. Credibility is one of those things you should work to establish early on.

The most beneficial way to do that is by developing and sharing strong and captivating content. See chapter seven, "Craft Your Content Like a Boss," for insight into how to produce content that builds trust and stimulates ongoing interest from consumers.

Brand Trust Matters

Brand trust isn't formed overnight and can be lost at any time. Consistency and promise go a long way in building trust, and trust breeds longevity.

> **People talk.** But beyond talking, people tweet. People Instagram. People Yelp.

The rise of social media sharing means that brands are now forced to be a lot more accountable than they've ever had to be before. Your brand is delivering a promise, and if you fail to meet that promise, the effects of social sharing can halt your business, or worse, impact your brand's reputation (and profit) long-term. Marketers refer to this as being customer-centric.

Customer-centric brands really (and I mean really) understand *their* people. Refer to chapter one, "Today's Consumer Mindset" for a refresher of people's basic expectations. Also, consider doing some research and creating profiles of who your ideal people are to help you figure out how to be sure you're meeting the correct needs and expectations. Brands that focus on customer satisfaction have more loyalty, get more referrals, see more repeat business, and are afforded greater word-of-mouth publicity. Your goal is to make sure that when you're not in the room, the discussions about your brand are favorable.

QUICK TIP: TAKE TIME TO CREATE BUYER PERSONAS

Personas are fictional representations that help depict a profile of your prospective people. Whether you're marketing to businesses or individuals, having a few personas on-hand will help you get a better understanding of the day-to-day life of your consumers.

BUYER PERSONAS: AT-A-GLANCE

Examples:

Joan, 36 years old, mom of two, wife, hectic home life, not a lot of extra cash to spend. Active on Facebook and Pinterest. Struggling to manage her weight. Interested in finding ways to fit a healthier lifestyle into her daily routine and increase her self-care.

Jason, 27 years old, always on his phone. Prefers to watch programs on YouTube instead of television. Attends lots of local sports events and concerts. Active on Instagram. Hates his job. Wants to make more money and enjoy his career. Looking to figure out what's next for him in life.

A WORTHWHILE READ
Book Recommendation

"Buyer Personas: How to Gain Insight Into Your Customer's Expectations, Align Your Marketing Strategies, and Win More Business." by Adele Revella

Personas aside, top brands spend lots of time and energy understanding what satisfaction *really* looks like to their consumers.

THE INS AND OUTS OF CUSTOMER SATISFACTION

Brand experience

Brand personalization

Brand accessibility

Brand Experience

Brand experience is just a fancy term that means people enjoy interacting with you. Brands with good (or great) experiences have done their research, so they know what their customers want and expect. Since they're committed to gaining loyalty, they do their best to make sure every interaction is positive. Brands with great experiences typically focus on keeping interactions simple and convenient.

Taking a look back at Jeff Bezos for a second, let's examine Amazon.

You can buy just about anything from Amazon, minus pets, spouses, or children (and I wouldn't be surprised if that changed soon), and with all of the items they sell, the website never feels cluttered or overwhelming. The search function is easy, they store your credit card details, they even remember the purchases you've made previously and allow you to go back and find your shopping specifics. Not to mention the one-click shopping. The *experience* of interacting with Amazon is easy.

Every brand's experience is different, and you shouldn't look to model your brand experience off of someone else's. Instead, focus on the connection that you want to have with your customers. Identify the emotions that you want your customers to feel after they've interacted with you. How you make people feel will keep you top-of-mind.

Experiences are rooted in emotion. If you want people to feel empowered or confident after interacting with your brand, then that becomes a staple in the experience of interacting with you. The experience should start on your website and continue through to your social media channels, as well as to any outreach efforts like emails or events.

Though your brand experience is an important element of differentiating yourself from other people, it's not something you need to stress about. When all is said is done, you know why you created your brand. Keep your *why* top of mind and frame out your brand experience to best explain *why you do what you do.*

Brand Personalization

When you say personalization, most non-marketers assume you're referring to addressing someone by their first name in an email promotion, when in fact brand personalization is so much more than that. Personalization is more about giving people more of the things they *want.*

Learning the little things your customers or followers care about and want to know about will help you develop smarter marketing campaigns. In the long-run, these insights also help you to be more profitable.

In order for personalization to work, you have to know *who* your customers are. Luckily, you've done some personas, so you better understand your consumers. Knowing things as simple as people's job responsibilities or stress level can help you better tailor your future messages.

Netflix does personalization quite well. The things you've watched previously shape the programs they tell you about in the future. This same theory can apply to you and your brand. If you're an esthetician and see that a client always comes to you for massages, that means they like body relaxation. In the future, you could personalize an offer for them based on knowing their habits. It could be something as simple as recommending a massage plus a body scrub at a special discount since they've already expressed an interest in body calming treatments.

Personalization requires you do some homework. You need to look at the habits of your customers (or ideal customers) and review what they've purchased (or expressed interest in). From there, you'll be able to tailor your products, services, and marketing communications to their individual preferences. For customers, there's nothing worse than a company that doesn't seem to know them. It makes you come off as someone that's not truly invested in them and only looking to get their money.

Brand Accessibility

Knowing that patience isn't today's consumers' strong suit, it's important that people be able to access you.

People get really frustrated when they feel like a brand is not accessible. That doesn't mean that you have to be available 24 hours a day, seven days a week. It means you need to clearly convey *when* and *how* people can reach you. For business ventures, simply letting people know what days and hours you are available can do wonders for painting you as trustworthy. When customers can't reach brands, they often go right to social media with their gripes. You never know when a bad review or interaction will be posted online or possibly even go viral. Safeguard your brand's reputation by making sure you communicate how and where people can find you.

KEEP CUSTOMERS HAPPY AND SATISFIED
Happy and satisfied consumers become repeat consumers and social media fans, then brand loyalists, and ultimately, they'll make up your brand tribe.

A 101 GUIDE FOR BUSINESS BRANDS

You MUST listen to your customers.

Your customers have feedback, and you *have* to listen to it. In fact, a best practice is to ask for it—a lot.

People like to be heard, so whether the feedback is good, bad, indifferent, or incomplete—every little bit helps you craft a more customer-centric experience and make sure that people *like* dealing with you.

Your customers MUST be able to reach you.

There's nothing more frustrating than not being able to reach someone at a business. Be sure you clearly state when and how your business can be contacted. If you happen to only accept inquiries via email or form, include a response time so that people know when to expect a callback or e-response.

You MUST respond to your customers.

When people have questions about your business, don't just leave them hanging. Sometimes this can be tricky on social media, primarily because questions often come in quickly, but do your best to be as responsive as possible. It may be best to instruct people to email if they have questions.

You MUST get to the bottom of any issues.

Leaving a customer issue unresolved can be disastrous. If a customer has an issue or concern, be sure to do your due diligence and get a good understanding of what happened and why it happened.

You MUST acknowledge your wrongdoing.

If the incident was something that's not so flattering to your brand, be sure to try and repair the experience as much as possible by apologizing to your customer and perhaps offering an incentive. This is not the time to save face, it's the time to make things right.

You MUST follow up.

Keeping your customer updated is essential for developing a successful brand. Let people know where things stand and follow up shortly after everything has been resolved.

Wrapping Things Up

Customer-centric brands, both personal and business, know the importance of satisfaction as a contributor to long-term success.

It's vital to keep people happy and engaged because happy people listen to you, tell others about you, and spend more money on you. They become brand ambassadors that keep coming back for more of your brand experience. Remember that your customers or social media followers can go away in a heartbeat. There's always an alternative to your brand; therefore it's important that you <u>always</u> operate with them in mind.

PART 2

Set the Stage
for Success

CHAPTER 4

Where You Fit In: Defining Your Brand

There isn't a brand alive that is all things to all people. *Not one.* We have way too many choices, options, and alternatives—and that's okay. With this in mind though, it's important that you narrow down who and what your brand is early in the game. Whether you're embarking on building your personal brand or your business, you need to be specific about who you are and who you're talking to.

Anyone who takes the leap to develop a brand is going to be wearing lots of hats and juggling multiple roles early on. At any given time, your role in your brand could vary. Some days you'll be the CEO, CFO, or customer service manager; other days you'll be the HR specialist, sales director, or lead researcher. Every day though, without fail, you *are* the marketer.

With lots on your plate (and your sanity often at stake), it becomes even more critical that you define your brand early on, to avoid costly and timely marketing mistakes that will eat away at your budget and frustrate you as you attempt to self-manage.

Taking time and committing to the brand development process will help you pinpoint the things you'll need to incorporate into your marketing to help ensure that people remember you.

Unfortunately, there is no way we'll be able to walk through every element of branding in one short chapter. So instead, this chapter will provide a high-level look at some of the key ingredients you should think about when positioning your brand out in the world.

BRANDING, 101

Branding (or brand development) is a series of components that helps identify **you**. A brand can identify an individual, product, or company. It includes things like your logo, tagline, and any symbols that represent you; but it also includes your value, voice, and promise. Proper brand development helps distinguish you to consumers and has a profound impact on whether or not people have an interest in interacting with you. As you develop your brand, these elements will shape everything from the types of content you develop to the way you talk to consumers.

Branding can be a difficult task, especially for large corporations and businesses. For individuals, entrepreneurs, and start-ups, however, it literally starts with you (the person)—but, before you can get others to buy into who you are, you first have to know who you are.

In the long-term, properly defining your brand will help you:

Earn respect.

The more you properly define your brand, you'll begin to see that your name starts to mean something to people. You will begin to become more trusted in your industry. Well-defined brands get more respect, more respect means a stronger brand reputation, and a strong brand reputation means more people will crave interacting with you.

Open the door for new opportunities.

Well-defined brands, whether they are personal or business, get a bevy of opportunities including things like speaking engagements, partnership requests, and media – in addition to more customers and clients.

Get endorsers and advocators.

As your brand becomes more defined and polished, you'll begin to see people advocating for you. One person introduces you to someone (often based solely on the strength of your branding), and that person knows someone else who knows someone else. Each advocator will help your brand become more influential and better-known. With that understanding, let's just jump right in.

WHERE DO YOU SHINE?

As the face of your brand, you've got to start by reflecting on who you are. Know that no one is good at everything — no one, but everyone is good at something. Your brand's foundation should focus on your strengths. The things you're good at will be your moneymakers in the future.

What are you good at?

You'll want to keep your strengths top-of-mind as you start branding yourself.

Managing and leading teams	Setting direction	Helping people overcome hardships
Budgeting	Selling	Communicating
Networking	Navigating technology	Building relationships
Teaching, training, or coaching	Managing and meeting deadlines	Getting people to their goals
Writing	Multitasking	Adapting to change
Telling stories	Planning events	Public speaking
Making people laugh	Getting people to think differently	Mentoring people

Improving processes	Solving complex problems	Getting people to listen to you

Use these things to help you generate ideas to differentiate yours from others.

Additionally, you'll want to infuse these strengths into your brand experience as you become more comfortable in who you are and what you represent. Your strengths can be incorporated into your brand in all types of ways, most notably through your content.

Keep this list in your back pocket. It will make it so much easier for you to determine the types of content that will best showcase these strengths. We dive into all things content marketing in chapter seven, "Craft Your Content Like a Boss." In the meantime, just make a note to remind yourself that your strengths and your content go hand-in-hand.

What do you stand for?

Next up, we have your personal convictions and values. As a brand, you'll need to identify the deep beliefs that are the driving force behind what you do. Marketers refer to these as your brand's core values.

These values define your personal views and clarify who your brand is to the world. Pretty much every major company has a set list of core values. Now it's time for you to define yours.

Try to keep them to four or less.

Compassion	Respect	Integrity
Community	Accountability	Quality
Diversity	Service	Collaboration
Commitment	Efficiency	Accuracy
Guidance	Partnership	Virtue
Beauty	Inclusivity	Fun
Education	Adaptability	Responsibility
Agility	Optimism	Professionalism

People can't read minds, so having core values will help you help consumers understand why your brand exists. People are more likely to get on board with brands that have similar core values to them.

QUICK TIP: PEOPLE WANT TO KNOW WHAT YOU STAND FOR AND WHY

There are countless ways to integrate your core values into your brand. For businesses, a simple (and common) way to share your *what* and *why* is to include a section on your website called "Core Values" that briefly lists them followed by 1-2 sentences that elaborate on why these are so important to you. For personal brands, try something like "what I stand for." Your core values can be incorporated into your social media pages in something as simple as your brand's profile description or in the "about me" section and also on your website.

What does your brand represent?

Start by asking yourself where you'd like to be in five years. Think about this as it relates to your brand or business. Then, look beyond where you personally see yourself and think about how you envision your brand impacting your industry. What do you want to have accomplished five years from today? This type of vision is essential as you think about what your brand will represent, not just now, but in the future.

What do *you* represent?
What's *your* personality?
What character traits do *you* embody?

Dependable	Energetic
Strategic	Driven
Passionate	Results-Oriented

Transparent	Innovative
Logical	Honest
Positive	Kind
Collaborative	Trustworthy
Disciplined	Self-Reliant
Generous	Ambitious

What is/are your area(s) of expertise?

Every brand falls into an industry based on its area of expertise, the type of products it sells, or the types of services it offers. In order to make your mark in your industry, you first have to define it. Identifying the categories that align with your area of expertise will help you better position your brand or business to stand out from other entities in your industry (e.g., your competition).

What categories does your brand fall into?

Try to keep them to one or two.

Health and Fitness	Project Management	PR or Communications
Research	Retail	Wellness
Human Resources	Marketing	Entertainment
Operations	Education	Hospitality
Transportation & Automotive	Housekeeping & Domestic	Finance & Accounting
Arts and Entertainment	Social Work	Law Enforcement/ Military

Counseling	Construction	Banking
Business Services	Computers & IT	Medical & Pharmaceuticals
Waste Management	Food Service	Activism & Non-Profit

Since your brand is a vessel of help, start thinking about how you'll use your expertise to help educate, entertain, and/or empower others. In this instance, as is true for much of marketing and branding, the best way for you to showcase your expertise and value will be through content. We deep dive into content more in chapter seven, "Craft Your Content Like a Boss," but for now, just remember that all the pieces interconnect.

The things you're good at connect to the things you stand for. The things you represent connect to your areas of expertise. Then, the things you enjoy connect to your brand personality. Let's look at how your personality intricately connects with the other key components in defining your brand.

YOUR INTERESTS AND PERSONALITY HELP DEFINE YOUR BRAND

As a personal brand or business owner, the things that you enjoy outside of work help give your brand some spunk. These are elements that humanize you and make you relatable to other people. Every brand (especially start-ups) needs to have a distinct personality in order to command attention. Once you've identified your interests, you can start to sprinkle parts of your personality into your brand to make you more memorable.

What do you enjoy (outside of work)?

Cooking	Fitness	Writing
Photography	Hiking	Sightseeing
Reading	Concerts and Music	Blogging
Knitting	Gardening	Camping/Fishing
Podcasting	Drawing	Sports
Volunteering	Movies	Meditation

What elements of your personality are you really proud of?

Incorporating these personality traits into your brand messages will enhance people's interest in you and provide a more complete picture of the *real* person behind the brand.

Creative	Funny	Confident
Patient	Geeky	Easygoing

Friendly	Silly	Brave
Kind	Respectful	Forgiving
Athletic	Dependable	Supportive
Organized	Loyal	Disciplined
Selfless	Helpful	Persuasive
Straightforward	Quick-witted	Reliable
Charismatic	Talkative	Authoritative
Strong	Sincere	Generous

Your personality and the things you enjoy are central to brand success through social media. We do a deep dive into social media as a key element for brand growth in chapter 8, "Successfully Navigating Social Media;" therefore I won't spend much time on it now. Just know that you'll need to become comfortable sharing the human elements that make you who you are in order to create deep connections with people. All of the above elements are characteristics that reflect who and what your brand is made of.

THINKING ABOUT YOUR BRAND IDENTITY

Now that you've identified what you stand for, what you represent, and the things you're good at and enjoy, you're ready to move on to the other components of branding that will give consumers a more complete picture of who you are. Marketers call this your brand identity. Most people actually start here and miss the entire first section of questions altogether, which are key in helping you find your differentiation. When combined, all of the above questions and below elements work together to make your brand more credible, relatable, likable, polished, and trustworthy.

Your Logo

Your logo is a word or symbol (or a combination of both) that helps people readily identify you. It's the <u>face</u> of your brand.

Does every personal brand need a logo?
No, certainly not.

A personal brand, as in Judith Washington, Tax Accountant, certainly does not need to spend time developing a logo. Allen Stuart, Professional Photographer, may, however. The reason is that Stuart's audience is likely very visual. As a photographer, his brand is creative, which means he could stand out more to his ideal consumers by adding some type of visual interest to his name. Washington, on the other hand, could probably create a successful brand simply with her name written in the most basic of fonts. This is where knowing your consumer, industry, and competition really come in handy. We talk more about this in the next chapter where we delve into strategy.

Rules for business brands, however, are a bit different.

Should a business have a logo?

Generally, yes.

However, it's important to remember that a logo is *not* your brand—it's simply one small element. Your logo is one of the first impressions of who your brand is. Keep your logo simple and don't use too many colors or fonts. Also, looking back at WIIFM for just a second, I want to note that your logo does not add any value to your consumer other than to show that you, in fact, are a business entity. Your logo is about you, not about "them," so it doesn't need to be huge, and it doesn't need to be the focus of your marketing. Instead, focus more on your message and your value, and end with a small logo to tie things back to your brand.

Your Tagline

Chances are you've heard about or seen a brand tagline. A tagline is a short and catchy statement that grabs people's attention.

Here are a few of the more notable examples:

- FedEx: "The World on Time"
- Bounty: "The Quicker Picker Upper"
- Nike: "Just Do It"
- Walmart: "Save Money, Live Better"

It's important to know that every brand does not need a tagline. Starbucks, for example, doesn't have one and look at all its impact. A lot of newbies get hung up on trying to find the perfect tagline or catchy hook, when it's often an unnecessary brand element, especially early on.

If you feel really strongly that your brand needs a tagline, be sure you keep it clear and concise. My recommendation, however: don't focus so much on crafting the perfect tagline, and instead focus on being a reliable and customer-centric resource that delivers on its word. That will get you farther than any slogan ever will.

Your Color Palette

The idea of colors in marketing can be controversial because everybody's preferences are different. Marketers do a ton of research to understand the psychology of colors in branding and consumer perception.

Moving away from the psychology of colors as an indicator of behavior, I recommend you start with the colors you like and go from there. No need to overcomplicate this. Start with two to three main colors that you want to represent you. Stick with those colors as your brand begins to take shape. That way you'll start to develop some consistency in your color palette and consumers will start identifying your brand with a specific style and set of colors. Ultimately, this is your brand personality, so you're allowed to define it however you want.

Your Voice, Tone, and Commitment

How your brand speaks to people is up to you. Voice and tone are other important elements that make up your brand's personality. In true marketing form, this is also a pretty complex subject matter, so I'll try to be concise.

Speaking personally for a minute, my "Keli Hammond" brand (both personal and professional brand) is friendly, passionate, informative, enthusiastic, and authoritative. That encompasses my brand's voice as well as its tone. How you plan to interact with your ideal consumer defines your voice and your tone.

For example, if your brand is geared towards teens, college students, or young adults, you may use slang in your messaging as part of the way to connect and relate to them. If you work in education or in academia, you may be more on the formal side. This is another reason why doing your research upfront is that much more important. Using the wrong tone to your consumers can cause them to look the other way or ignore you altogether.

Your brand voice is very closely tied to the elements of your personality that you identified earlier in this chapter.

BRAND VOICE VS. BRAND TONE

Examples of voice can be fun, serious, friendly, passionate, cheerful, concerned, reliable, or practical. Your brand's tone, however, may be expressed as laidback, professional, edgy, sarcastic, or even formal.

Refer back to your core values and what you represent. Your brand can be serious or humorous. It's all defined by what *you* stand for and who *you* are as a person. Start with how you (yourself) talk and go from there.

GOOD BRANDING STARTS WITH IDENTIFYING *YOUR* STRENGTHS

From there you're able to be more intentional in how you promote those strengths. Before your marketing will resonate, you must have a solid brand foundation that knows what it stands for and represents. Another major element in brand development is personal branding. See chapter 11, "Brand Yourself for Demand," and combine the takeaways from each chapter to help you create your winning brand formula.

Wrapping Things Up

Branding is a huge part of differentiation, and differentiation is what makes one brand or business stand out from another. It shapes how people see you. This isn't a section to skip in the brand-building process. Doing the work here will help guide you so that you're more intentional, deliberate, and cohesive in how you present your brand to the public. Your goal is longevity, and longevity starts with defining yourself at a deep level.

CHAPTER 5

What's Brand Growth Without a Strategy?

I haven't met an entrepreneur or influencer yet that has said, "Nope, I don't want more business or opportunity." I haven't heard anyone say, "no thanks, I don't need to make more profit. I'm good, don't send me any more customers." It's usually the exact opposite. Everyone wants to know the recipe for profit. People want to know how to monetize their ideas, skills, and interests. Think back to chapter two, "Today's Consumer Mindset," for just a second. Do you recall where we talked about how skeptical the consumers of today are? That skepticism is the main reason brands need a clear and concrete strategy for marketing. The concept of a marketing strategy is one of the more challenging components of this field. There are even marketers who struggle with it. Most people are much better identifying and employing what marketers refer to as tactics—advertisements and promotions that talk about products and services —and they miss the strategy piece altogether.

Examples of marketing tactics are an email you send out, a blog post you write and publish, a video or podcast you create, a photo you share, a Google advertisement you run, an event you hold, a webinar you host, and a postcard you distribute. <u>Tactics are the individual things you do in your quest to let people know that you have a product, service, or resource</u>.

Tactics are promotions or actions, but tactics are *not* strategy.

Don't get me wrong, tactics are essential elements of marketing. Think of them as <u>tools</u> in your toolbox. But without a toolbox to hold the tools, you'd have things scattered everywhere, unorganized with no order. Strategy is the box you keep everything together in. Without a strategy tied to your tactics, your brand will only be successful in the short-term. Longevity requires strategy first.

Strategy is clarity about your long-term vision. It's your game plan, your blueprint.

Your tactics then fall under your strategy and are aligned to your larger brand vision. If you remember nothing else, remember that every successful brand starts with a good strategy. They then determine their marketing tactics and timing within that strategy.

YOUR STRATEGY STARTS WITH YOUR GOALS

Goals are incredibly important in the brand-building process because they help clarify your vision. Clear goals help you identify where you want to take your brand, and by what time, and include a step-by-step process of how to plan to get there.

GOALS, DEMYSTIFIED

Your long-term goals will form the foundation of your strategy. This is your big-picture dream that you want for your future-self.

Your short-term brand goals are things you'd like to begin or accomplish soon (say within the next 12 months). Your long-term brand goals, on the other hand, are the things you'd like to achieve in the next 5-10 years.

In order for things to take shape, you have to write your goals down, then visualize the steps you need to get you there. My recommendation is to identify both, then shift your focus more to your short-term goals. These are going to be more attainable in your mind because your long-term goals will be big. Sometimes they're so big they scare you, so I write them down and come back to focusing on your short-term goals. These are the things you can visualize happening over the next several months.

Examples of Short-Term Goals	Examples of Long-Term Goals
Find a personal trainer and start working out twice a week, every week. Each workout should be at least one hour.	Lose 90 pounds and fit into the dress I wore to my 10-year class reunion.
Enroll in a management certification program and complete at least 4 of the 8 required courses by June 30 of this year.	Get out of a support role and into leadership (become a department director) even if that means switching employers.
Develop five problem-solving, tutorial videos and post them online. Upload them all to Instagram and YouTube by three months from today.	Become a full-time, paid, professional speaker.

Your short-term and long-term goals work together, so focusing more on your short-term goals still moves you closer to the big goals. Goals help you stay on track and keep you laser-focused when things get chaotic.

Years ago I worked with a gentleman who had dreams of becoming a sought-after comedian. He was working an office job as a research analyst but had hopes of shifting himself into comedy superstardom. He reached out for assistance in goal setting and brand strategy since he was trying to pivot into a completely different career.

Since he was a complete unknown in the world of comedy, I suggested that one of his short-term goals be to start creating videos of himself in skits and posting them online and to his social media pages. We agreed that he would develop four skits a week for the next six months so that he had a portfolio of content that showed what he was capable of. For his long-term goals, he ultimately wanted to get on television (in any capacity) as long as it allowed him to showcase his comedic funny bone.

Less than two years after determining his goals, he was making enough money doing comedy to support himself without his research job. At the four-and-a-half year mark, he had over 700,000 followers on social media. Just after reaching the sixth anniversary of this first time we sat down and wrote out his goals, he got a message from a producer at a top cable network that wanted to talk about casting him in an upcoming show.

Goals help you frame your dreams and put shape around the foundations you need in place to make them happen. Within the goals, write down the small daily changes you'll need to make and things you'll need to prioritize. Be sure you are specific in every goal you create for yourself.

Let's say you already have a business. Your short-term goal might be to increase the number of people that visit your website and fill out your "contact" form. More completed contact forms mean more leads that you can talk to and try to persuade to become customers. Your long-term goal could be to bring in $1 million from your email promotions over the next five years.

SETTING GOALS FOR YOURSELF AND YOUR BRAND CAN BE CHALLENGING.

Examples of common brand goals are:

» Get more people and traffic to my website
» Get more people reading my blog
» Get more subscribers to my newsletter
» Get more customers buying my products
» Get more followers to my social media channels
» Get more reviews from happy customers
» Launch new products to expand my portfolio
» Make more people aware of my brand

> **Your brand goals can be whatever you want, but the best goals contain specifics.**

They should identify not only the goal itself but also state *when* the goal should be achieved by. It's important to add times around your goals to help you keep up your momentum. Another element that should be included in your brand goals are measurements that will help you determine when the goal has been met.

For example: If you want to get more subscribers to your blog, your goal(s) could be something like: "Develop a free downloadable workbook on [specified topic] by [specified date]. Use that resource to entice people to subscribe to my blog. The ultimate goal is to have 2,000 new blog subscribers by April 30 of next year."

QUICK TIP: ADD LOTS OF DETAIL

When thinking about your brand goals, specifics matter. Be detailed in timing, process and the outcomes you seek. The more specific the goal, the better. For your short-term goals, always add a completion date, it will help you stay the course along the way. Long-term goals should be big, but not impossible. Think about your ultimate brand or lifestyle dream; that's likely your long-term goal.

Let's say Jon's goal as a brand owner is to increase the number of people who visit his website and fill out the "contact" form. Let's frame this brand a bit more to really dive into this goal.

> Jon owns a catering business and is preparing his brand for the upcoming holiday season. He wants to focus on Thanksgiving, Christmas, and New Year's as his biggest areas of opportunity. His short-term goal is to get people to his website so that they see the full scope of his catering

services and ultimately choose his company to provide their food services.

It's September, so Jon has decided that he's going to take those two months and build up his portfolio so that when people visit his website, they're immediately captivated and their mouths water. He's decided that he will add 10 new food pictures a week to his website. He's also going to start sharing some of his recipes on his website.

To make sure he doesn't overwhelm himself, he's only going to post two recipes a month. Lastly, since he already uses social media, Jon is going to post pictures of his food and talk about his recipes on his social media pages.

All of these things will serve as the foundation of his brand strategy, and they all started with his goals. Once your short-term and long-term goals are done, you can really dive into your strategy.

STEP 1:
DO YOUR RESEARCH

Marketers refer to this section as market research, but technical terms aside, this is the stage where you really get to know *your* industry. If you're serious about building a successful brand within your industry, you need to know *all* about it.

Since market research is such a massive part of marketing and can take you down so many different roads, I suggest you keep it simple and start here.

1. Does the industry/market need your product?

a. *Why* does your industry need your product or service?

_____

_____

b. *How* do you know for certain?

_____

_____

2. Do your products/services meet the needs of consumers?

a. How do you know? [Revisit chapter two, "Today's Consumer Mindset."]

3. What are your consumers struggling with?

a. What shapes their need for your product or service?

_____

_____

4. Are your fees/prices in line with what else is being offered?

a. Are you lower, higher, or about the same?

b. Who in your industry charges more/less than you do (for similar services)?

Service 1: Their Price: _____ Your Price: _____
Product/Service: _____

Service 2: Their Price: _____ Your Price: _____
Product/Service: _____

Service 3: Their Price: _____ Your Price: _____
Product/Service: _____

Service 4: Their Price: _____ Your Price: _____
Product/Service: _____

Service 5: Their Price: _____ Your Price: _____
Product/Service: _____

If you have an already established brand or business, it's also useful to hear from your past and existing customers. This will help you gather intel into how people see your brand in the marketplace. Try sending a survey, holding one-on-one interviews, or doing a small focus group (no more than 10 people) to get insight on how your customers feel about your brand. If you do interviews, be sure to record them so that you can go back and transcribe the information and further dig into the responses.

STEP 2:
CHECK OUT YOUR COMPETITION

Everybody has competition. In chapter one, "The Beliefs and Mindsets Behind Craved Brands," I stated that your mindset should be that you are your only competition. Of course, that's a metaphor to keep you focused, but in real business, there's real competition. That means it's important that you know *all* about what your competition is doing.

You're not looking to copy, but rather to understand their behaviors. If you don't know what your competition is up to, you can't stay ahead of them. It's that simple. Marketers call this a competitive analysis, and we don't dare start a project without a comprehensive one.

1. How long has your competitors' brand been around?

2. How do they define their brand mission, vision, and purpose?

3. Who are they targeting (and how do you know)?

4. How do they promote their business?

   a. Do they have a website? [List the site address]

   b. Do they have a blog? [List the site address]

   c. What are their social media pages? [List all that you come across]

      i. How big is their following?

      ii. Who are their influential followers?

      iii. Who are their most engaged followers? [commenters, frequent likers]

5. Have they had any media attention?

   a. Where and when?

6. What's in their portfolio of products, services, or resources? [This may not always be listed, depending on the industry. For example, consultants don't typically list their prices

anywhere. The cost is project-based, and thus not promoted. Regardless, see what you can find.]

7. Do they offer a lot of promotions and special offers?

    i. If so, how frequently and what's the typical discount?

8. Do they have members or a club?

    a. How much does this cost, and what is the structure (meaning do people pay monthly or is it an annual one-time fee)?

This section could go on forever. Start with these questions and adapt as you start to look around and learn more about what your competition is up to.

QUICK TIP: START SNOOPING

Dissect everything your competition does. Doing a thorough competitive analysis will serve as the backbone for a lot of your decision-making. Select no less than five competitors, no more than 10.

STEP 3:
DETERMINE YOUR TARGET CONSUMERS
[ALSO KNOWN AS YOUR TARGET AUDIENCE]

Marketers use the term target audience to refer to the people you want to influence in any way. These are the people (or groups) that you hope notice you and become your customers or followers.

Everyone is not your target audience. If you've already started developing your buyer personas (discussed in chapter three), then you're already on the right path to thinking about your target audience.

The easiest way to determine your target audience is to identify the people who will benefit the most from what you offer. If you sell organic baby diapers, for example, the group that would benefit most from your product is expecting and new moms. If you own a local coffee shop, your target consumer might be residents, businesses, and tourists in the area.

In an effort to help you keep your sanity during this process, I won't go into the nuances of in-depth research that is often involved in marketing (demographics, psychographics, and behavioral studies). Just like everything else, it's highly technical, and even though marketers tend to enjoy it, it's super detailed and can be overwhelming.

Instead, below are some questions that you should know about your audience (regardless of your goals or industry).

» What's their age range?
» What's their gender?
» What's their race or ethnicity?
» How much education do they have?
   High school, college, advanced degree?
» Are they typically married or single?
   Are they the head of the household, or a spouse?
» What's their average household income?
» Do they typically have children?
» Do they generally have a religious affiliation? If so, which one(s)?
» Where do they live?
» What do they like to do in their spare time?
» Where do they eat?
» Where do they shop?
» What types of music do they listen to?
» What's their preferred political party?
» What people do they follow on social media?

Knowing these details will help you determine where to find your tribe of people and understand how best to connect with and talk to them.

STEP 4:
DEFINE YOUR MESSAGE

So now you should have a pretty good understanding of your industry, competitors, and target audiences. Next up, your key messages. These will determine how you communicate with your target audiences.

When you think about your brand's message, go back to your long-term goals. Think about the impact you want to make on your industry.

Remembering chapter three, "The Customer's the Boss," it's important that your brand's key messages help inform people of what you do and connect the dots between WIIFM and how your brand helps address problems. You can have multiple brand messages, but keep them short and sweet because people are impatient and will stop listening.

WHEN CRAFTING YOUR BRAND MESSAGES:

Don't be stuffy.

A good rule of thumb is to write the same way you talk. Also, don't be afraid to show the more humorous and light-hearted parts of yourself. These things humanize you, and people will begin to identify you and relate to you based on how you write and speak. Relax a little. No need to be so polished that you are unapproachable.

Don't say the same things your competitors are saying.

Originality will always win the race. Sure, it's ok to be inspired, but, certainly don't copy the things you see. Do your own thing, and say what's on your mind. You can take the same concept that your competition has and talk about it in a completely different way. Switch your wording up, and be creative in how to relate to popular topics and current events.

Don't be long-winded.

Being too wordy or long-winded is a surefire way to ensure people stop listening. Focus on being brief and succinct. If you have an outline of what you plan to talk about, there's no reason that you should be talking for 20 minutes when you can get your point across in five. As a reminder, consumers are impatient. They want to hear what you have to say, but they also want you to get to the point.

Going back to the example about Jon, his key message might be something like:

> As an on-demand chef, I am committed to helping you save time and enjoy delicious and healthy meals without the hassle of cooking.

> My business makes it easy for people to eat healthy and affordably by offering organic meals delivered right to your door.

STEP 5:
DEFINE HOW YOU'LL PROMOTE YOUR BRAND

You have your goals, you've done your research, you've identified your competitors, you know your audience and key messages, so now it's time to decide how you're going to promote your brand.

We're back at marketing tactics—the promotional part of marketing. Tactics are what most people think marketing solely consists of. I hope that you're seeing that marketing is in fact so much more than this. Not long-ago brand promotion only centered around your website. These days, your website is a key component, but it's often social media that sparks the real interest. It's still important, however, that you get people to your website because it's a huge part of being seen as credible and trustworthy by skeptical consumers. So, with your website as the backbone of your promotion, you can focus on the specific promotional elements that your brand is going to use to talk to the world.

What will it be?

- ☐ Television & Radio
- ☐ Print Advertising (Magazines/ Newspapers)
- ☐ Social Media
- ☐ Email
- ☐ Search Engine Optimization (SEO)
- ☐ Search Engines Marketing (SEM) [Google + Bing Marketing]
- ☐ Events

- ☐ Content Marketing
- ☐ Video
- ☐ Influencers
- ☐ Mobile Texts
- ☐ Word-of-Mouth
- ☐ Cold Calling/ Telemarketing
- ☐ Podcasts
- ☐ Media Tours & Promotional Events
- ☐ Webinars/Live Video Streams

For newbies, your budget for marketing is typically pretty limited because you're trying to juggle and manage so many different elements of your brand.

If this is the case for you, you can cross off television (note: local television stations often offer deep discounts and special offers for regional programming). You can also probably cross off print advertising like magazines, but everything else is fair game.

For cost-conscious brand builders, future influencers, and early-in-the game entrepreneurs, your best go-tos are:

> » in-person and online networking and relationship building

> » sharing unique and interesting content online through various channels

> » being present and active on social media

Networking.

Tell everyone you talk to about your personal brand or your business. Remember, however, that good marketing is not about you, it's about other people. Make sure you frame your self-promotion to showcase what you do for others. Practice starting your brand sentence with "I help..."

Examples:

I help people beautify their homes and enjoy the spaces they live in.	Interior Designer
I help single moms confidently re-enter the dating world after a divorce.	Matchmaker
I help people improve their credit and save money so that they can move into homeownership.	Financial Advisor
I help people ensure their book manuscripts flow, read well, and are error-free.	Freelance Editor

Content.

Besides word-of-mouth, **content serves as the lifeblood for effectively marketing your brand**, regardless of how big or small your marketing budget may be. Content, also referred to as content marketing, is your brand's best opportunity to educate, inspire, or entertain, while quickly building your credibility and showing your expertise. Content is also a great way to showcase your [brand] personality to mass amounts of people quickly. It's how people organically find you through search engines like Google and YouTube.

Content includes everything from the photos you take and post to the videos you create and share – and good, shareable content is a big part of the secret-sauce to brand success. Content really is your best friend. I talk in depth about developing strong content in chapter seven, "Craft Your Content Like a Boss," but since this is such an important element of marketing success, I wanted to touch on it quickly.

Now, back to tactics for a moment. As far as your determining your brand's marketing tactics, start by selecting no more than three or four categories from the list provided on page 124.

YOU CAN'T FORGET ABOUT SOCIAL MEDIA

Social media is another major part of brand success. However, it's not enough to just be present on social sites, you need strong content. Once you've finished chapter seven, chapter eight goes into the ins and outs of how your brand can use social media and see massive growth, get more likes, more comments, and more followers, all of which increases your brand's exposure.

IDENTIFY HOW YOU'LL MEASURE YOUR SUCCESS

In marketing, we're all about measuring our activities to see how well our marketing efforts perform. We refer to them as marketing metrics or key performance indicators (KPIs). The purpose of metrics and KPIs is to help you identify whether you should keep doing what you're doing or if you should switch things up to see bigger results. Our goal is always to market smarter, not harder.

YES, YOU NEED TO TRACK AND MEASURE THE THINGS YOU DO

Metrics and KPIs are incredibly important in marketing, regardless of your goals. Knowing how well your marketing campaigns, content, and promotions are working will help you pivot or restrategize if something is not performing how you'd hoped.

Metrics and KPIs are yet another part of the ever-complex field of marketing. So instead of going through every nuance for calculating the performance of your promotional efforts, I've identified some activities that you can easily track to gauge your marketing suc-cess.

Leads and Prospects	The number of strangers who express interest in learning more about your brand.
Revenue, Profit, or Cost	The amount of money you make during a set period of time.
Retention	The amount of repeat custom-ers (or upsells) you see.
General Engagement	The number of people who see your brand as meaningful and worthwhile (often these are the people who interact with your brand through your website, social media, or email).
Awareness	The number of people who become aware of your brand as the result of a specific activity (e.g., from being a vendor at an event).
Search Engine Optimization (SEO) Traffic	The number of people that find your website organically through search engines like Google, Bing, and Yahoo!.
Social Media Engagement	The number of people that click or visit your website as a result of finding you on social media.

To keep things simple and because there is a lot to digest, start with your brand goals and align your metrics with those. For example, say your goal is to increase website visits from your social media profile. Your metric may be to get 50 clicks on your web address from your LinkedIn page within a month's time span. Metrics are designed to help you see if what you're doing is effective so that you can change your approach if it's not. No one wants to waste their time, so I encourage you to add metrics to your goals so that you periodically check in on your marketing progress.

QUICK TIP: UTILIZE TRACKING TOOLS

If you haven't already done it, add Google Analytics to your website. It's free, simple and will give you tons of great insight into what people are actually doing when they get to your website, including the pages visited most frequently, average amount of time spent on your site, and what areas visitors reside in. Social sites also offer tracking tools that help you monitor interactions, engagement, and clicks. Beyond the free tools, there are countless resources to help you monitor your brand.

THE PATH TO PURCHASERS: WHAT GETS CONSUMERS TO BUY?

Marketing is both an art and a science. The ultimate goal of all marketing is to **change** someone's behavior [in your favor], which could mean that you want someone to click a link, download a resource, order a product, watch a video, request a service, attend an event, or simply share a post.

Regardless of what it is, you want people to do something for you. That's a tough job. You have to find people at the *right* time, and you have to say the *right* things in the *right* tone.

To do that, marketers infuse a mix of research, psychology, sociology, anthropology, human resources, and economics into our work with the goal of seeing the *maximum* return for all we've done. What we've learned as technology has evolved is that in-your-face advertising and salesy slogans don't cut it like they used to.

In order to build a highly-successful brand in today's market, you no longer have to use the more traditional advertising methods like television, radio, magazines, and billboards to get people to buy into you. So, what does it really take to convince someone to hear you out?

What Gets Today's Consumers to Buy Into a Brand?

People want a friend's (or an influencer's) stamp of approval.	People want to see reviews from past customers or users.	People want to watch videos of brand owners telling their stories.
People want things personalized based on what they like.	People want to know a brand's purpose and the reason why they exist.	People want reasonable prices for your products and services.
People want special offers and discounts in exchange for their patronage.	People want to see unique and authentic content that is interesting and relatable.	People want to be rewarded for their loyalty and allegiance with special programs.

A Friend's [or Influencer's] Stamp of Approval

Think restaurants for a second. How many times has one of your friends come to you raving about how good their meal was from the new Thai spot they checked out over the weekend? Sometimes they describe it so well that you go and make your reservation while they're still talking. Stamping something as good (better yet, outstanding) can do wonders for a brand. Friends are an easy place to start.

An influencer, on the other hand, can be brand gold when it comes to getting in front of large amounts of people quickly. How influencer marketing works can be tough to understand, but I talk more about it in chapter eight, "Successfully Navigating Social Media."

Reviews from Past Customers

Customer reviews are another way to get sincere and authentic stamps of approval. The modern-day, highly-skeptical consumer wants to know that other people like or trust a brand before moving forward. Look at the success of websites like Yelp and TripAdvisor, and you'll see just how powerful reviews can be in influencing decisions. Focus on getting a variety of testimonials, and then be sure to add them to your website and to social media platforms like LinkedIn.

GET TOP REVIEWS & TESTIMONIALS

In order to get high-quality reviews, be sure you're providing a top-notch brand experience from start to finish. The same way a *good* stamp of approval helps a brand, a *bad* stamp can severely hurt a brand.

Videos

Want people to remember you? Add some videos to the mix. Because this is one of the most impactful ways to transform a brand from unknown to unrivaled, I've dedicated all of chapter nine to video marketing. For a comprehensive look at how to incorporate various types of videos into your brand's strategy, thoroughly read through that chapter.

Personalization

Because the consumers of today are primarily interested in knowing what's in it for them, personalization is a really powerful way to show people that you've been paying attention to them. Top companies spend millions of dollars each year on consumer personalization.

For a novice, personalization can be done, it just takes a little more forethought and effort. Use all of the research you have done thus far to help you really understand who your consumers are. The things you discover will help you develop content that is more personalized to the wants and needs of the people you're trying to influence.

Knowing a Brand's Purpose

Your brand's purpose and the passion behind why you do what you do can be a game changer. This starts with *you* opening up and letting people know what *you* stand for. This is where you pull the core values you developed in chapter four.

The best way to share your purpose and core values is by opening up and telling your brand story. I've dedicated an entire chapter to this part of brand building. We dive into this in chapter six, "Captivate and Connect with Your Brand Story."

Price, Price, Price

Prices typically matter to consumers but not always. Luxury brands, for example, don't have to worry so much about pricing. For most other brands, personal and business alike, your price matters.

Doing your research and knowing your competitors will help you determine the best prices for products, services and collaborations. To determine your prices, you'll need to ask yourself how much your consumers are willing to pay for that type of service. You'll also need to be sure your prices are in-line with your competitors.

The quality of your products also plays a role in how you price yourself. Pricing can vary greatly from one brand to another depending on the cost of materials, labor and overhead (e.g., office space). In the end though, customers still have the expectation of getting the best deal they can.

Special Offers and Discounts

People love a good sale, discount, or special offer. However, it's important that you don't make this the foundation of your brand. Don't discount yourself or your contribution to your industry because that then becomes who you are—the discounted brand that's always on sale.

Using special offers or discounts should be done sparingly and at times that tie into your audience's needs. For example, if your target consumers are moms, doing a "Back to School" special offer could be a great idea for your brand.

Be mindful of what your competitors are charging, but ultimately form your price structure around the research you pulled earlier in the brand strategy planning process.

Unique and Authentic Content

Content is how top brands and businesses showcase their expertise and skills. By creating valuable, helpful, and relevant content in a variety of forms, successful brands earn trust and strong reputations among masses of people. This helps position them as thought-leaders and invites more profit and influence. We take an in-depth look and explore all things *content* in chapter seven, "Craft Your Content Like a Boss."

Loyalty Programs

People love to feel like they have access to something others don't. That exclusivity is an advantage that brands in all industries and of all sizes can take advantage of.

Perhaps creating a loyalty program could help differentiate you from your competitors and increase long-term retention from your consumers. This is also a good way to let your customers or supporters in on the things you're doing ahead of everyone else. Think about if you want to offer special discounts, coupons, select access, or perhaps advanced buying specials. Loyalty programs can be a brand's best friend.

Wrapping Things Up

Strategy is a critical part of building a successful brand, and it's something that many people fail to focus on. When you don't think about how you'll use all of your tools in your toolbox, it becomes much harder to build a foundation that lends itself to longevity.

Before jumping into your market, spend time on your goals, do your research, know how you'll identify your success, and truly understand the people you're trying to influence.

PART 3

The Key Ingredients in the Secret-Sauce

CHAPTER 6

Captivate and Connect With Your Brand Story

Everyone's distracted. And impatient, and forgetful, and overwhelmed, and busy, and has a super-short attention span. In the midst of that, however, they're still reading blogs, scrolling social media, watching videos on YouTube, and searching Google like there's no tomorrow. People are listening.

But what are people listening to?

The answer is: people are listening to stories.

Expensive, flashy television ads don't get people's attention like they used to. All the advertising glitz and glam that once allowed big corporations to own entire markets is gone. Today, people want a more human experience that they can genuinely connect with and relate to. They'd prefer to see *real* people as opposed to fancy, big-budget, salesy ads.

Enter...you.

People want to hear about who you are, where you came from, and how you got to where you are. They want to listen to *your* story. That includes your wins, losses, ups and downs, failures, setbacks, and triumphs. They want to reminisce with you, and laugh with you, and admire you, and walk through life with you.

Your unique and personal experiences are the things that set _your_ brand apart from everyone else's.

Did you recently get married?
Okay, tell us about it.

Did you recently try a product, go on a fun road trip, or read a new book?
Okay, give us the details.

Was getting laid off what inspired you to start your own business?
Okay, tell us how you made things happen for yourself.

Was growing up in foster care what set the stage for you becoming a mentor and freelance counselor? Okay, walk us through the experiences that shaped you.

One of the best things about brand storytelling is that it works for anyone, in any industry, with any goals, at any time.

STORIES MAKE YOU MEMORABLE

Well told stories help you build deeper connections that make people not only stop and listen but also remember you.

Stories are a distraction that people readily embrace. We will scroll right past your sales pitch video, mute your shameless product-of-the-month plug, and completely ignore your three-for-the-price-of-two flyer; but switch your approach to telling stories instead of pitching, and we're captivated.

But why?

It's because stories make you human. They make you relatable. They inspire our minds and give us new ways of thinking about situations.

GOOD STORIES ARE FOUR THINGS

Good stories are focused.	Good stories are memorable.
Good stories are entertaining.	Good stories are relatable.

Focused.

You have about seven seconds to get people's attention, and that number is shrinking. On social media, it's often less. That means your story needs to have a purpose. It's important for anyone telling a story to know *why* people need to hear it. If a story is unfocused and difficult to follow, people stop listening and move on to the next thing. So, being focused, succinct, and well-organized will help ensure that your story doesn't jump around.

GOLDEN RULE: one character (you)* + one incident (plot) + one outcome (ending)

---

*In instances where your brand is a joint venture, one character may become your collective group of founders or co-founders.

Memorable.

Storytelling gives you the opportunity to create lasting impressions. This is an opportunity for your personality to shine. Our brains long to know how people got to where they are. Once people have heard a memorable story, they forever connect it with the person that told it (in this case, your brand). Oftentimes people even remember details and can recall specific statements that were made.

Entertaining.

One of the most effective ways to tell entertaining stories is to tie them to real human feelings and emotions. Tell stories that make people happy, angry, sad, scared, or surprised—if you're evoking an emotion, people will be entertained. You want people to put themselves in the room because they are so connected to the things you're saying.

Relatable.

Your story won't relate to everyone, and that's okay. But it is a best practice to try and tell stories that are as universal as possible, meaning it has the potential to connect and resonate with the largest audience possible. That includes talking about overcoming obstacles, going from rags to riches, recalling incidents that changed your perspective, or unlearning old habits. Relatability starts by talking about your feelings and being genuine.

WHY SHOULD YOU TELL YOUR STORY?

First, stories give your brand energy. You're able to tie in your personality, tone, and voice, and really just be you.

Second, people want to share and be inspired by your resilience. There have been things that tried to deter you from your path. There have been life experiences that you learned a great deal from. There have been tough times, great times, and everything in between. Sharing these experiences through stories will not only help people connect to you, it will draw them in because they will find immediate connections between their story and yours.

People are looking for inspiration to help them overcome life challenges, open up new possibilities and personal directions, and transform how they see their futures in the world. Stories take people away from their daily routines, even if only briefly, and give them a chance to see the world through a different lens.

START THINKING ABOUT THE THINGS THAT HAVE SHAPED YOUR LIFE

By telling your personal story, you have an opportunity to help people find their purpose. When your story inspires someone, they feel more connected and are more likely to listen to what you have to say.

WHAT MAKES FOR GOOD STORIES?

Everyone has a story, but **not everyone shares that story in a way that adds value to their brand**. The narrative and delivery of your story are equally as important as the story itself.

When thinking about how you'll differentiate your brand through storytelling, remember the following.

It doesn't have an ego.	It shows a sense of vulnerability.	It showcases resilience.
It is honest and genuine.	It challenges people to think differently.	It is transparent and open.

Good stories are ego-free.

Before you can tell a good story, you have to self-reflect and check your ego at the door. Even the most successful person in the highest leadership position has room for improvement and has made mistakes. The best stories don't only focus on where you are now, they walk people through the past and show how far you've come.

Another good rule of thumb for telling ego-free stories is to share credit with others. Who helped get you to where you are? Did a family member or mentor inspire you or change your life in some way? If so, it's good to incorporate some of those details into your story.

Good stories are honest.

The authenticity and truth behind your stories matter. Just as you wouldn't want a relationship full of lies and dishonesty, the same rules apply for your stories.

Don't be afraid to face the truth head-on. Plus, being upfront, open, and honest about the things that have shaped you will open the door for others to feel comfortable telling their truths and moving forward despite setbacks or uncertainty.

Good stories showcase resilience.

Adversity and difficult times hit us all at some point in our lives. You never know what someone is going through or how your experiences can help them overcome tough times. Sharing some of the struggles, challenges, and setbacks you've experienced often spark light in others and connect them to you in ways you never imagined possible.

The less-than-pretty parts of our lives are often the parts that we want to omit when telling stories, but those are the parts that show us as human. No one is perfect, so no one can identify with someone who has never been through tough times. Talk about how you adapted. Share strategies that can help other people that may be going through similar situations.

Good stories challenge people to think differently.

Some of the best brand stories share your thoughts, your feelings, and your mindset. Think interview-style stories. Taking those thoughts and transforming them into stories could mean you talk about anything from life lessons and personal situations to roadblocks and shifting your perspectives. Like some of the greatest movies ever written, great stories challenge people to think differently.

Encourage people to take a stand against the status quo. Perhaps you have a story about reinventing yourself after adopting a new way of looking at life. If so, tell people about it. They may want to shift too!

Good stories show a sense of vulnerability.

A lot of people think of vulnerability as weakness, when it's actually one of the greatest testaments to courage. Being emotionally exposed in your stories leads to deeper connections and more trust.

Consumers are drawn to people who are down-to-earth and imperfect. Vulnerability displays bravery and shows you're fully uncensored in sharing the things that shaped you.

Good stories include a level of transparency.

Get in front of things that may not have been so perfect in your past. Transparency in storytelling piggybacks on honesty and vulnerability but also includes an openness to be willing to speak your truth even if it contains things that aren't so pleasant. Just keep in mind that there's no need to tell the world everything about you since birth, just the things that help connect you to the good you're now doing in the world.

WHERE TO START

DECIDE WHAT KIND OF STORY YOU'RE TELLING

There are different types of stories that you can tell as you begin crafting your brand strategies.

Give people an inside look at who you are.	Talk to people about how you overcame a hardship.	Walk people through how you got to where you are today.

TELL YOUR STORIES THE SAME WAY YOU WOULD IF YOU WERE TALKING TO A FRIEND

Stories should be **conversational**, regardless of the type you're telling. You want people to know that you've struggled and endured the same things they have. Talk as if you're catching up with a close friend or colleague.

QUICK TIP: STORYTELLING IS NOT AN ADVERTISEMENT OR SALES PITCH

Like everything else, storytelling is not about your brand. It's about your life. Don't sell, just talk. Any story you share should always be a selfless act designed to connect people to the experiences that have shaped you.

WAYS TO TELL YOUR STORY

Write it.
These are your blog posts, books, and articles.

Speak it.
These are your presentations, panels, and conferences.

Record it.
These are your photos and videos.

BEST WAYS TO CAPTURE ATTENTION

Tell Inspirational Stories

In order for your story to be inspirational, it has to include some vulnerability. You have to figuratively let your hair down and let people into the things that make you who you are.

The goal of your story is to get people to connect with you and identify with the things you've had to overcome and the hurdles that you've faced. In the end, you'll show your perseverance and help uplift people.

Tell Educational Stories

Educational stories are a great way to share your knowledge and get people to see different perspectives. The popularity of TED Talks is the perfect testament to great educational stories. These talks, which focus on innovative and creative thinking, spark global conversations around technology, entertainment, and design, and are globally known for the slogan "Ideas Worth Spreading."

Tell Lighthearted Stories

Entertaining stories tend to be more lighthearted. They often center around pop culture, comedy, modern-day trends, or your personal thoughts or perspectives. Entertaining stories make us zone out for a moment and take us away from the stress and anxiety of daily life.

LOOKING FOR STORYTELLING INSPIRATION?

A few business brands that knock storytelling out of the park are World Wildlife Fund, TOMS®, TED Talks, and Nike.

Some individuals that have built influential personal brands by combining great stories into their personal brands include yoga teacher and body positive advocate, Jessamyn Stanley, and makeup maven Huda Kattan.

Wrapping Things Up

Whatever types of stories you decide to tell should go hand in hand with your brand goals and what your target audience is looking to hear about.

Telling stories works equally as well for personal brands as it does for businesses. Be sure that your stories incorporate *your* voice, tone, and personality because you want people to start to get familiar with who you are as an individual and not *just* as a brand.

CHAPTER 7

Craft Your Content Like a Boss

Talk to any good marketer about marketing, and the word "content" will undoubtedly come up, and it will come up frequently. In our world, the phrase "content is king" is a regular part of daily conversation because, well, *content is king.*

Even though I'm admittedly tired of hearing that phrase, it's the absolute truth. That is, at least for the foreseeable future.

But, what is "content?"

Are "content" and "content marketing" synonymous? Whatever it is, how do you use it to elevate your brand and grow your exposure?

What is content marketing?

Content marketing is the process of *strategically* developing materials that promote your expertise (whatever that may be). These materials are developed with the intent to attract a certain group of people to you, and then proceed to educate, inspire, or entertain them.

In other words, **content is information** [related to your brand] that provides some form of value to consumers. Every picture, tweet, video, blog post, email, Instagram or Snapchat story, rant, opinion, and webpage that you share is considered content.

Content marketing is not a brand promotion, or advertising, or a pitch. However, when done right, good content gets your brand more sales, opportunities, connections, loyalty, recognition, and profit. It also helps build your brand's credibility, showcases you as an expert, and positions you to have more influence in your industry.

Content is a word you hear a lot in marketing, but before you start thinking about ways to craft really great content (this is the content that continually grabs people's attention), I think it's best to start by clarifying outbound vs. inbound marketing. These terms form the foundation of how content is developed, shared, and ultimately *discovered* by other people.

OUTBOUND VS. INBOUND MARKETING

To marketers, these terms and categories help us determine our strategies and identify the best areas of opportunity for brand growth. Outbound marketing, simply put, is marketing that *intrudes* and *interrupts* people. This type of marketing doesn't care what you're doing; it's going to push its way through to the surface and make you see or hear it.

When you think of outbound marketing, think radio and television ads first and foremost. You could be listening to your favorite songs or watching your favorite show, but when it's time for a commercial break, it's time for a commercial break. **Pause:** insert a series of unwanted interruptions.

Outbound marketing is *pushed out* to people, hence the term—outbound. Beyond radio and television commercials, outbound marketing includes some of our longtime favorites like telemarketing, newspaper and magazine ads, as well as billboards. As technology has evolved, so has outbound marketing. You know those banner ads you see as you browse your favorite websites? Those are also considered outbound marketing tactics. At one time, outbound marketing was marketing—in its entirety. That was the only way that brands thought they'd be able to sell their products. You had to push them in people's faces—literally making sure they heard or saw the promotion.

But, do people *really* see these ads? Years of research showed that consumers often couldn't recall the promotions. It turned out there were simply too many ads, and people stopped paying attention altogether. Brands were losing money and brand content was being ignored.

ENTER INBOUND MARKETING

Inbound marketing is just as the name suggests. It means that a brand has done something to pull people in and capture their attention, making them want to learn more. Inbound marketing is a lot less intrusive than outbound marketing, but it requires *a lot* more creativity.

Because inbound marketing isn't being shoved into people's faces, it has to be clever, compelling, and interesting enough to make someone *want* to watch, read, or click a link. The theory behind good content is that if you have a deep understanding of who your consumer is (meaning you've done thorough research), your brand can develop and distribute content in various formats that continually intrigue people. Inbound marketing can be seen most prevalently in blogs, social media, and email promotion.

In case you hadn't guessed it, inbound marketing is really just another term for content marketing. It means that a brand is using a variety of methods to try to fill a void for people so that they (metaphorically) come *in* for more information.

"In" can be anywhere. It can be people coming into your website. It can be people coming into your social media page. It could be someone getting an email and coming into the email to actually read the details.

So, back to content for a minute. In defining content, I wish that I could say that content was one thing. It would be so much easier to wrap your head around. Ambiguous is an understatement.

Just think of content as anything you produce for an audience that connects them to your expertise. It informs, educates or amuses them.

CONTENT EXAMPLES:
AT-A-GLANCE

▷ Articles
▷ Blog Posts
▷ Polls, Surveys, and Quizzes
▷ Case Studies
▷ Templates
▷ Videos
▷ Webinars
▷ Interviews
▷ Memes
▷ Research
▷ Screenshots, Emails, and Texts
▷ Quotes
▷ Charts and Graphs
▷ E-Books
▷ Frequently Asked Questions (FAQs)
▷ Personal Stories
▷ Photos
▷ Podcasts
▷ Checklists
▷ Tips, Tricks, and Tools
▷ Contests and Challenges

Content marketing is developing and putting out information that people *want* to read, watch, or engage with. Think back to chapter two, "Today's Consumer Mindset." Nowadays everyone is busy, impatient, and easily turned off, which are really just nice terms to say that they have commitment issues. These modern-day commitment-phobes aren't going to pay attention to things they don't find interesting. That includes brands (pretty much all of them), even yours.

It includes your products, your services, and your expertise. People just won't notice you. That is, unless your content is memorable. This low-commitment means you need to get your content right, or you run the risk or turning consumers off or being cast aside. Modern-day turnoffs for brands include unfollows or blocks on social media, unsubscribes to emails, or just flat out being ignored. So, in the infamous words of marketing experts everywhere—**content *really* is king**.

WHAT MAKES FOR GOOD CONTENT?

The first rule of thumb when creating content is, <u>good content isn't salesy</u>. Don't use your face time to promote yourself or your brand, use it to show people you know what you're talking about. Your goal is to show people that you're the real deal.

THINK OF CONTENT AS YOUR OPPORTUNITY TO SHOW YOU KNOW YOUR STUFF

Instead of selling yourself, prove yourself. Prove to people that you know what you're talking about by sharing your knowledge.

People are skeptical and hate being sold to. Not to mention, they're busy and inundated with life stuff, which means they don't have time for things they perceive as nonsense. It doesn't matter how amazing your brand or products are—if your content doesn't introduce them properly, you'll never get the result you're looking for.

Instead, people prefer you to walk them through something (a process, a situation, a scenario, a technique, or a story), and from there, they'll feel informed and more in-the-know. They like their questions answered and their problems solved, without it being arrogant, and certainly without it being boring. Above all else, your goal as a brand is for your content to show *how* you improve someone's life.

The things that we think improve us and add value to our lives vary from person to person, so something that improves person A's life is not the same thing that improves person B's life. Since life improvement is highly subjective, doing your research on your target audience beforehand will give you a real advantage and help you identify what to highlight in your content.

For example, someone may feel like their life is most enriched through their appearance. For these people, brands that focus on apparel, beauty, health and fitness, hair care, and wellness can thrive when positioned correctly. Someone else may feel more fulfilled in life through learning and exploration. In this case, brands that center around things like education, art, travel, technology and finance would be more appealing to this audience.

Whatever *your* people are interested in, those are the things that your content should address. Focus on sharing, connecting, and solving. This will take your brand farther than any "buy my product" pitch ever will. It's also good practice to get in the habit of continually reminding yourself that good marketing *never* centers around you and that people want things that help them help themselves.

IN TODAY'S COMPETITIVE MARKET, BRANDS THAT INCORPORATE STRONG CONTENT SEE MORE PROFIT

Having content is no longer an option if you want to be successful in your marketing efforts. Regardless of your focus, industry, target audience, or goals, content marketing makes the difference and gives you a real brand advantage.

FIVE FACTORS TO CREATING GAME-CHANGING CONTENT

The honesty factor.

Think about it. Brand building aside, who doesn't love honesty? If you were dating someone, you'd want them to be honest with you, and the same is true for brands.

> Honesty = trust and likeability = loyalty

When people trust you, they connect to you differently—and that connection is what's going to build you a following that looks to you when they need a resource, product, or service.

Honesty in branding includes candid conversations, open dialogue, and above all else—realness. It means real stories, real people, real scenarios, real circumstances, real environments, and real vulnerability. Your magic potion is *your* truth.

The passion factor.

Your passion for why you do what you do matters more than most people know—and there's a personal story behind that why. Showing that passion, showing other people how much you care about something makes them care. Passion cannot be faked, so don't try. People will see right through the phony stuff (maybe not right away, but in time), and they'll lose faith in you. So, before you embark on trying to connect and form a bond, make sure you actually love what you do and mean what you say.

Make sure you aren't just doing something to try and make money. If money is the sole reason you're seeking to build your brand, you can expect to struggle to connect with people long-term, not to mention you'll likely burn-out quicker.

The unique factor.

What makes your brand unique and original? Even if you do something that a million other people do; the experience you create will never be the same as theirs. Plus, the story behind *how* you got to where you are, is yours alone.

Marketers refer to this as brand differentiation or your unique selling proposition (USP). A USP is less about selling and more about defining and showcasing the things that make you different. Don't focus on being the best; focus on being different and unique.

The human factor.

Humans aren't robots, so good marketing isn't robotic. Strong content doesn't focus on perfection. In fact, it shows flaws and is humble and relatable. You're human, so remember to *be* human in your content.

> People are inspired by the imperfect.

Developing content that showcases your imperfections makes you more relatable because everyone knows nobody's perfect.

When you're able to show that you understand and empathize with the things people are going through, people are much more likely to connect with you.

The relevant factor.

When things are relevant, people identify with them. It speaks to who they are. Relevance is determined by your target consumer, which means you really need to know who you're talking to. See chapter five, "What's Brand Growth Without a Strategy" to help you develop more relevant content.

HURRY UP AND GET TO THE POINT

Everyone's time is limited, so people want you to get to the point, and fast. When you write or talk too much, you lose people's attention. In thinking about your content, shorter is generally better. Find a way to be informative without being too wordy or long-winded.

THE DREADED B WORD: BLOG

So many people are afraid of the word blog. It's not nearly as scary as it sounds. Nor does it have to take up an enormous amount of your time. Blogging is an easy way to let people know how you think and show what you're good at. Plus, you don't have to become an official blogger to blog. You just have to start writing or talking.

Most people want proof of who you are and what you do before they commit, and blogging (even just simply having a few articles on your website) helps show people your thoughts and expertise.

Start by identifying five topics that you can speak on. They can literally be anything. Then, just start writing or talking. In addition to blogging, you can also share your thoughts by vlogging (video blogging). An easy place to start is with a series of 'how-tos' or even simply by giving your opinions.

CONTENT GOLD: STORYTELLING

Should you use your content to tell stories? Absolutely. Think about your favorite movies. When you're watching a good movie, you are captivated. You connect with the characters and their struggles, you listen closely to every word they say, and you want to know how it ends. Your eyes are glued to the screen.

The same formula that works for movies works for marketing. Stories breathe life into your brand and add an even more unique factor to your content. They are your firsthand account of something memorable that happened to you and capture how that event changed you.

Every memory and conversation in your head is an opportunity to create interesting and personalized brand content. Plus, *you* get to decide how you tell it. Perhaps you create a personal blog. Maybe you decide to make a funny skit that people laugh at. Perhaps it's a short video that tells people what not to do in a certain situation. Revisit chapter six for a refresher on crafting stories people **crave.**

CONTENT RULES

Write It How You'd Say It

One of your most valuable assets is your brand's tone. Your tone is your brand's disposition or the personality that you want to put out in the world. How you naturally speak and interact should be carried through to your brand's content, whether it's in print or online, for consistency. Your brand is an extension of you, the person—not you, the robot.

It's Okay to Invite People In
(in fact, it's essential)

Unlike outbound marketing, inbound marketing isn't a one-way street. As you talk and share content, invite people to chime in and talk back. Good content starts discussions, and discussions help other people discover your work. The more people feel like they can talk to you, the more engaged they become. Not to mention, you'll find that your followers, subscribers, customers, and prospects have some great advice and helpful tidbits to offer. Some of the best brand ideas come from open dialogue and candid discussion.

Decide Where Your Content Will Live
(and how you'll distribute it)

Once you've determined the types of content you're going to produce, you need to figure out how you plan to share it with the world (and how frequently). Common ways to share content include your website, social media channels, emails, and other sites that are looking for content creators.

The best place to share your content is anywhere that you have existing connections. If that place is Facebook, then start there. Say you write an article on "how to start your own paint parties." Since your goal is for people to read that article, you have to let people know that it's available and link them to the webpage or video where they can get your advice. Point people exactly where you want them to go.

Wrapping Things Up

Who you are, what you know, and what you're good at are all important elements in how you can create great content. You either know how to make people smile more, or feel better about themselves (or laugh), or become a better person, or look better, or forget about their problems, or feel cooler, or be more in the know, or be more comfortable with who they are.

Whatever it is about you that improves the lives of others, is where you should start as you frame out your content marketing plan. Good content not only keeps people's attention, but also positions you as trustworthy, competent, likable, relatable and reliable—and what brand doesn't want that?

CHAPTER 8

Successfully Navigating Social Media

These days it's quite possible to build a brand empire solely by marketing yourself on social media. To try and deny the influence of social media platforms on the world would be a huge mistake. They have transformed modern-day communication.

Not only are people using social media to stay in touch with friends and family, they're also getting their news, learning new skills, listening to other people's opinions, watching videos, shopping, and connecting with strangers. In 2018, the number of people on social sites topped 2 billion, and that number continues to rise.

Anything that has over 2 billion users a year is some-where your brand should be. It's not uncommon to meet someone, and the first thing they ask is, "are you on social media?" followed by, "what's your Twitter, Instagram, or LinkedIn?" It's not just about staying in touch with family anymore; it's about staying con-nected to the world-at-large. For anyone looking to build or grow a brand, social media offers massive opportunities for visibility.

But, are there <u>rules</u> to brand success through so-cial media? I wouldn't call them rules, per se. Strat-egies for success and maximum impact—absolutely.

QUICK TIP: SOCIAL MEDIA IS **NOT** FOR SELLING

Even though *technically* you are promoting something, whether it be yourself or your products, on social media, it's best not to go in with a sales mentality.

Just because social sites aren't designed for selling doesn't mean that brands and businesses don't thrive there, because they absolutely do. It just requires some forethought and a firm understanding of social dos and don'ts in order for these platforms to work in your brand's favor. When done right, social media increases awareness of your brand, attracts new customers, grows your network, and ultimately brings your brand more opportunities.

SOCIAL MEDIA = ENTERTAINMENT

It's a place people go to interact, share, and collaborate. It's to be used for helping, inspiring, and telling stories—but not for selling.

Use it instead to showcase your brand's personality, beliefs, and viewpoints. Except for a few outliers like LinkedIn, social media is a place where people kick back, unwind, relax, and scroll. They don't want to hear you pitch your latest product or gadget.

Instead, use these platforms as an opportunity to connect and interact with people. Use them to build a community of people with similar interests and goals. Social media is designed for humans, not for businesses, which means that if you show the human side of your brand, you will see much higher engagement.

SOCIAL MEDIA MARKETING, DEMYSTIFIED

Social media is a place people go to have human interaction; it is not a place people go to hear about all the great products your business sells. The minute you start selling and pitching products, people stop listening and swipe away.

Instead, people want to relax and use these platforms as a way to fill up idle time, get new ideas, reduce stress, share their opinions, and make human connections.

So, what does that mean?

It means that if you have a product or service you'd like people to know about, it is most effective if you show the benefits of it, rather than selling the product itself.

HOW SUCCESSFUL BRANDS AMPLIFY THEMSELVES ON SOCIAL MEDIA

Every day there's a new brand vying for attention on social media. Some brands have millions of followers (or connections), while others have hundreds. Some are personal brands, and others are businesses. The one constant is that people are out in the world actively seeking to get noticed through these platforms.

Is it possible?

Absolutely. In fact, social media should be part of your brand strategy, as it's great for both networking and quickly getting in front of new audiences.

Nearly every week, I'm flooded with questions about social media marketing. Most people are either entrepreneurs, bloggers, or business leaders that are looking to use social platforms to get noticed. Most of them are already on social sites, but they don't have the traction they seek.

One thing I regularly see, from both my clients and people I interact with, is how impressed they are by brands with thousands of likes or millions of followers. So many people seek to emulate that "demand." Likes and followers, however, don't always equate to profits, opportunities, or brand ambassadors. Sometimes they are *just* likes and *just* followers. Though a large follower base *could* mean huge brand-related checks each month or a steady flow of new clients, that's certainly not always the case.

The key to building and monetizing your brand through social media lies less in the number of connections and more in how well you *actually* connect with people.

The secret ingredient to brand success through social media is your engagement, not your total number of followers, or the total number of likes you get per post. Rule of thumb: **focus less on the likes and more on the connections**.

ENGAGEMENT = SOCIAL GOLD

Social media is conversational, and just as users of these sites are conversing, your brand should be too. That means you should be talking, responding, sharing, and commenting on social discussions and trending topics.

You need to take the time to actively engage with people if you want social media to work for your brand. This is especially important for personal brands and newbie entrepreneurs. In order for people to get to know you, you've got to actually interact. This includes following people, sharing their content, and chatting. Social media will only work for you if you're social.

As you start refining your brand's social media strategy, remember that you're not there to sell; instead, you're there to connect and interact with a community that sees life the same way you do. The experience of each interaction will do your selling for you. People expect one of three things when they get onto their favorite social media site. They expect to be entertained, educated, and/or inspired. Nothing more, nothing less.

In order to effectively entertain, educate, and/or inspire people, you need to understand what your target audience is doing on social media. Without this insight, you're less likely to develop the types of content that speak their language. Social platforms are *global* online communities, and in order for your brand to be welcomed into these communities, you can't forget to show the human(s) behind the brand.

QUICK TIP: AUTHENTICITY IS YOUR SUPERPOWER

You, in all your glory, are what's going to help your brand stand out on social media. Just be you, whoever you are. Now is the time to get comfortable sharing your thoughts.

WHO DO YOU WANT TO BE ON SOCIAL MEDIA?

POSITIONING YOUR BRAND

Be a SME, Industry Expert, or Authority Figure

You know a lot about a lot. Consider using your social media page to position yourself as a subject matter expert, industry expert, authority figure, or coach that shares expertise on a specific topic in your field. Share your personal stories, insights, and ideas, and help people understand how they'd benefit from having you in their corner.

Freelance Your Services

If you're looking to offer freelance services, social media is a great way to get your talents in front of new potential clients. It can help you find opportunities and supplement your income. Use your social page to show and share your skill set and showcase your capabilities.

Earn Extra Money Through Affiliate Marketing

Affiliate marketing is you teaming up with a company and posting about their products or services and earning a commission as a result. For every sale tied to you, you're able to make some additional money. If a brand is targeting the same audience that you have access to, it's a great way for you both to benefit.

DO YOU SELL AN ACTUAL PRODUCT?

USE OR WEAR YOUR PRODUCTS AND TAG THEM

If you sell items or offer services, social media is a great way to highlight your offerings. Be sure that you tag the website or include the link to buy or learn more.

TIME AND SOCIAL MEDIA

It's important to be mindful that for any social media endeavors you decide to take on, you will need to dedicate time planning, preparing and posting content that keeps your brand top of mind for consumers.

Social media platforms are not the place for infrequent communication. They require ongoing monitoring and interaction; otherwise, you run the risk of losing traction or posting with no real return.

SOCIAL MEDIA FOR BUSINESS: WHERE SHOULD YOUR BRAND BE?

All social media sites aren't created equal. Also, some are better for growing brands than others. Use this list to help you as you think about which platforms you'll use to set the stage to grow your influence. No need to get on all of them; one or two is a great way to start familiarizing yourself with what works best for you based on your goals.

FACEBOOK

Facebook still reigns supreme as the most popular social media platform in the world. For brands and businesses, Facebook offers the opportunity to create dedicated business pages where you can share content, links, photos, and videos. Facebook is not a stuffy site, so make sure your brand is personable, friendly, and approachable. This is a platform where people feel like they can let their hair down and relax a little, and they have that same expectation of brands and businesses.

THINGS TO KNOW:
✓ Facebook has a ton of advertising

options to help brands increase their awareness. The ads are straightforward to set up and even let you test to see if one is more engaging (or well-received) than another.

✓ It's really easy to grow your following. If you've set up your brand with a business page, every time someone likes that page, they automatically become a follower of yours.

✓ Facebook allows you to promote (or boost) your posts, offer unique contests with incentives for participation, and do live streaming videos; all of which increase brand engagement.

✓ Facebook is one of the best places to grow your brand organically, which means it's easy to get your posts in front of massive amounts of people without spending a dime.

TWITTER

Twitter moves fast. Really fast. In marketing, we refer to Twitter as a microblogging site, which means that it's a platform where people share super-short posts about any and everything happening in the world. It's a place people go to share random thoughts or get quick bursts of news. Though this makes for some fascinating and creative content, it means it's easy to get overwhelmed and get lost in the Twitter rabbit hole. Content overload is likely imminent.

THINGS TO KNOW:

✓ Twitter will require a lot from you but offers enormous opportunities for brand exposure. Just get ready to post often. People bounce in and out of Twitter, and because of the volume of content, you'll have to post regularly to increase the chances of people seeing your posts.

✓ You'll want to use one of the free tools that Twitter offers that allows you to shorten your website links (e.g., Bit.ly) because you'll need the room. Twitter's short character count makes it a really unique social platform but having less space can sometimes be more of a challenge.

✓ Quick-witted, light-hearted, and

funny posts will do wonders for your engagement on Twitter. Twitter users love a sharp tongue, GIF file, and meme.

✓ Avoid sending automatic responses to people that follow you. They are impersonal and don't seem genuine. Plus, they're likely to be ignored or turn people off.

INSTAGRAM

Instagram is all things photo and video. Owned by Facebook, Instagram offers a visual look into people's lives. You can (and should) add captions, filters, location tags and hashtags to your posts to increase who sees them. You should also use features like Instagram stories and live video to share your life behind the scenes.

THINGS TO KNOW:

✓ Your Instagram profile and the description of who you are matters big time. Good profiles tell people the incentive of following you. Be creative and clever but also informative. You're selling, but not selling (if that makes sense).

✓ As a brand, whatever you promise to be in your Instagram bio should be conveyed in your photos and videos. Otherwise, you will confuse people, and they'll either retreat and stop connecting with you or unfollow you altogether.

✓ On Instagram, more than other social platforms, it's important to be clear and cohesive in the content you post. Instagram shows your content in a feed of three posts per line, which gives visitors an immediate at-a-glance look at the style and quality of your content; and quality matters. Be sure your photos and videos are clear and the picture quality is good.

✓ Hashtag, hashtag, and hashtag some more. The quickest way to expand who sees your posts on Instagram is through hashtagging. People from all over the world click hashtags for inspiration and to get ideas. You can open massive opportunities by continually incorporating and diversifying your hashtags. Good hashtags can even help your photo or video go viral.

PINTEREST

Pinterest is another visual platform, just like Instagram, but it works very differently. Pinterest curates its content in a completely different way than Instagram, calling its content "pins." The sole purpose of each pin is to share ideas and inspiration. These pins can also link directly to your website or any specific web page you'd like. You can find just about anything on this platform from recipes and home décor to DIY projects and tattoo designs.

THINGS TO KNOW:

✓ Pinterest allows you the option of automatically pinning existing content like blog posts or articles that you've written, making it much easier for you to grow your brand's visibility through this platform. Additionally, they offer the option of including "Pin It" buttons on e-commerce pages, which makes sharing products easier.

✓ Pinterest has a very advanced search functionality that makes it easy to find your competitors and see what's working well for them, and seeing the types of content that works for them will help you improve your brand content moving forward.

✓ Knowing the trending topics and keywords your consumers are searching for (and adding them to your content tags) can significantly increase your pins' visibility and brand's exposure.

✓ Pinterest offers group boards, which is a great way for brands to collaborate and share similar types of content. It'll get your pins in front of loads of new people.

LINKEDIN

LinkedIn is a site designed for professional networking. It's a place where business professionals meet and connect. LinkedIn is a great way to expand your network and is especially useful for building your personal brand. It's an opportunity to showcase your strengths, capabilities, and past work experience. It's really more of living/breathing resume or CV and can do wonders for helping validate your credibility.

THINGS TO KNOW:

✓ Don't use your brand logo on this

platform; instead, use a picture of yourself. The same is true of your name. Use your actual name, not your company name. On LinkedIn, it's all about you—the person, the professional, not your business. Note that LinkedIn does allow you to create specialized business pages, and that would be the place to include your brand's logo.

✓ Your headline offers an opportunity for you to make a dynamic first impression. Sprinkle in some buzzwords that show you know what you're talking about within your industry. This isn't the time to showcase yourself as clever; this is the time to showcase yourself as qualified.

✓ It's a great place to pile up your recommendations, which will be helpful in backing your brand reputation. Ask your friends, current or past coworkers, and clients to weigh in on working with you. People can also endorse your skill sets, which helps to persuade others of your brand's value.

✓ A good way to start building virtual

networks is to join some LinkedIn groups and start commenting on posts. As with any social media site, being social is the name of the game. Even though LinkedIn is all business, it's still a site designed for social interaction. As such, you should be posting, commenting, and liking just as you would on any other social media platform.

SNAPCHAT

Snapchat is a social messaging app where people quickly share photos and videos without much thought or time invested. It's a click and send it kind of site. Snapchat refers to its photos and videos as "snaps," and they disappear just minutes after they are viewed. Some photos and videos can remain viewable for up to 24 hours, but after that point, the content expires.

THINGS TO KNOW:

✓ Snapchat's feed shares content in a way that makes storytelling incredibly easy. If you decide to use Snapchat for your brand, you'll want to remember to continually post because your content won't be visible 24 hours after you share it.

✓ The most effective way for a brand to leverage Snapchat for marketing is by taking advantage of their advertising opportunities. It's an inexpensive way to get your brand content front and center to large groups of people you seek to target.

✓ Besides paid advertising, Snapchat is great for doing behind-the-scenes looks or sneak peeks of what your brand is up to. It's also a great way to tease products that you'll soon launch by sharing product tidbits and teasers.

✓ Snapchat is considered a cool and hip social platform so your brand will be seen as trendy if you use it. However, if that's not part of your brand strategy or if your target audience doesn't frequent this platform, then it may not be the best option for you.

YOUTUBE

YouTube is the second most popular social media site overall, ranking just behind Facebook in popularity. It's a video-streaming platform that hosts videos on any and everything you could ever imagine. YouTube is the holy grail of influence, turning unknown everyday people into celebrities. Whereas other sites give you a page or feed, YouTube gives you a channel, and that channel becomes the home for all of your content.

THINGS TO KNOW:

✓ Scripting your videos is important, or at least having an overall list of clear talking points to help keep your videos focused.

✓ You can do any kind of video you want—your brand, your decision. Popular video types include explainer videos, product reviews, interviews, and how-tos.

✓ Don't use your video to ask people to buy your products or services. Instead, tell people what you think or show them how to do something. Your expertise and knowledge base is your biggest asset.

✓ YouTube makes it really easy to add your videos to your website (or other people's websites) which helps you get more views, shares, and visibility.

✓ People can (and do) create playlists of videos they like or find valuable, which means that anyone who sees that playlist will encounter your video.

THE POWER OF INFLUENCE: AN INSIDE LOOK AT INFLUENCER MARKETING

Dictionary.com defines influence as: "the capacity to have an effect on the character, development, or behavior of someone or something, or the effect itself."

As social networking sites have become a driving force in how people connect and communicate, we've seen a new phenomenon emerge—**enter the influencer**.

Influencers, also called brand ambassadors, are dominating digital platforms like Instagram, Twitter, and YouTube by continually finding creative ways to inspire, empower, and exchange information with massive groups of their engaged followers. Everything they post is impactful and gets tons of views or shares. Because we're already on our phones all the time, it's only natural that marketers would find a way to leverage this as a means to grow brands.

Good influencers help brands get more website and social media traffic, more viewers of their posts, and [typically] more product sales. These are people that have built *authentic* connections with their followers, and as such, their followers have grown to deeply trust and value their opinions. An influencer's endorsement of a brand is a stamp of approval, and that stamp can do wonders for brand growth.

THE NEW CELEBRITY: THE INFLUENCER

Influencers represent a whole new type of celebrity. Through their personal connections, brands can leverage influencers' relationships with their audiences, which can open brands up to a much wider range of people.

Looking generationally at behavior, millennials and generation Z'ers aren't just swiping their phones to see the latest selfies and restaurant photos, they are *actively* deciding what to buy and where to go, courtesy of their favorite influencers.

Elevating Your Brand's Visibility Through Influencer Marketing

Think of influencer marketing as a brand partnership, where the influencers' values and target audiences align with your business strategy. The influencer comes in, adds their personal touch and voice to your product or service, then posts to *their* social media page, creating an opportunity for entirely new dimensions of brand exposure.

Because influencers are regular people, many consumers are more likely to trust them. Even with consumers becoming more skeptical overall, influencer marketing continues to be seen as credible and trustworthy.

There are certain industries that are capitalizing on the power of influencer marketing more than others. Cosmetics, luxury, clothing and sports brands have their pulses on influencer marketing. It's not uncommon to see top companies like Sephora, Nordstrom, and Puma employing a network of influencer affiliations to promote their goods.

SOCIAL MEDIA:
KEY SUCCESS INGREDIENTS

✓ Most of the sites I've listed have business functionalities. If the platform offers a business profile, regardless of whether you are a personal brand or have a business, you should be set up with a business profile. You'll want to have access to insights to help you improve your future content.

✓ Social media needs constant love and attention. Constant. Check your sites daily—starting in the morning and then again in the afternoon or evening. Get in the habit of doing regular pulse checks to ensure you're staying in-the-know.

✓ Make sure your brand is showing its human side, and it's not all business and advertising.

✓ Be intentional about the content you post. Make sure your content aligns with the core values that you and your brand stand for.

✓ Don't forget that customer service still exists even when you're on social media. Respond to business inquiries that you get in a timely manner, regardless of whether you're a personal brand or have a business. If you'd prefer that people email you instead of messaging you through the social platform, no worries, just let people know that.

✓ Make sure you're being social. It's called *social* media for a reason.

✓ Learn from your existing content. If something worked well, continue to replicate it going forward.

✓ Your social media channels should all connect to one another (whenever possible). For example, connect your Facebook with your Instagram, your LinkedIn to your Twitter, and so on.

✓ If you plan to offer special offers and promotions through social media (which you should if you have tangible products), create specific coupon codes for each channel to help you monitor the success of your promotional efforts.

✓ Tie your content to news stories or trending topics whenever possible. They make your brand seem more in-the-know. This will also help you better connect with and engage a new follower base.

✓ Incorporating strong hooks that encourage people to take a specific action can work wonders. In marketing, we refer to this as the "Call to Action," and it's an opportunity to direct people to *exactly* what you want them to do.

> Here are a few examples:
> o "Register for my new master class to learn the steps you need to write a best-selling book."
> o "Download my new eBook for tips on how to make vegan-friendly meals in under 15 minutes."
> o "Listen to my latest podcast for details on how to get your brand on TV."
> o "Tag a friend who loves ice cream as much as you do."

✓ Start some discussions on your social media pages. People love giving their opinion. Ask people what they think about a hot topic or upcoming popular event. Social media is a great way for brands and businesses to connect with people by asking them to chime in or answer quick questions on the spot.

✓ Show admiration to the people that interact with you online. These are the people that deserve extra attention because they're invested in your brand. Show them some virtual love by commenting and posting under their pictures and videos as well.

✓ Remember, we live in a visual world. Make sure the content you associate with your brand is high-quality, looks professional, and aligns with your brand personality.

✓ Many social media sites have sophisticated algorithms running behind the scenes that determine who sees your content and who doesn't. These algorithms are updated often, which means your brand needs to stay active if you want to maximize your exposure.

Wrapping Things Up

The goal of social media is to share your life as it's happening. It's designed to be used in real-time. That same concept applies to businesses and brands.

Remember, you don't need to be on every social site; in fact, depending on the brand, one strategically captivating social page can do the trick of five average pages. Start with conversations, get involved in trending topics, and watch how your engagement improves.

CHAPTER 9

Using Video to Revolutionize Your Brand

Want someone to remember you and your brand? Video is the best way to make that happen. Videos are quite possibly the most effective way to inspire other people, tell your stories, and share your experiences. Videos make us laugh, they make us think, they make us cry; but most importantly, they capture our brains in a way that makes us *remember*. Videos fascinate us.

Think about all the movies you love and the people that make those movies memorable. It's because they combine visuals and audio, which allow us to look at mannerisms, hear tone, see body language—but most importantly, see emotion. Emotion is a huge part of forming deep connections with people.

Although YouTube ranks just behind Facebook in total users, trends and surveys show that YouTube is actually the *most popular* social media platform in America. Another stat worth noting is that people watch over 1 billion hours of video content via YouTube every single day.

But, for a lot of people, the thought of doing brand videos is intimidating. Where do you start, and what kinds of videos should you make? It's important to remember that video is *one* of many marketing tactics in your toolbox; it just happens to be one of the most useful to build your brand's visibility and tell your story.

DETERMINING THE GOALS OF YOUR BRAND'S VIDEO MARKETING

The reasons for developing a brand video can be vast. Your video can be anything you want. Your content, your decision.

> » Maybe your business is growing and is looking to convince people that working for you is a good idea. You could create a video about company culture that walks people through what it's like to work with you.

» Perhaps your business is hosting an event. You could create a video of the event and the attendees interacting with each other to help give future attendees an idea of what they can expect should they attend.

» Maybe you want to show someone how a product works. You could do a tutorial video that walks people step-by-step through a process.

» What if you want to give people an idea of what it's like to have you as a coach? You could develop a video where people share testimonials about the experience of interacting and working with you.

QUICK TIP: PEOPLE WANT TO SEE REAL EMOTION

Videos skip all the fluff and cut right to two of our key senses—sight and sound. They make it easier for us to captivate people because they help us showcase our confidence, personality and poise.

Here's how to connect the dots between brand storytelling and video. Since you've already done the work of identifying where your brand fits in (courtesy of chapter four), this will help you form a solid foundation of things that you should bring forth in your videos. Refer to your core values along with the things you identified as your strengths. From there, you're ready to start thinking about which types of videos you should produce.

A BRAND BUILDER'S VIDEO MARKETING CHEATSHEET

How-Tos And Tutorials

"How To" videos are just what they sound like. They involve you teaching someone how to do something. What kind of something? Practically anything. You can be teaching people an actual craft, or you might be teaching people how to think differently. Both are equally valuable and equally sought out. My favorite how-to videos are makeup tutorials or videos that show me how to do something correctly like a workout routine or household project.

Think about your target consumer and what they may need help with; center your how-tos around providing them clarity and solving their problems.

Other popular how-tos involve teaching someone how to transition from one thing to another. For example: How to Become a Travel Blogger.

Event Promos or Recaps

People want to know what to expect before they commit, primarily because they are inherently skeptical. So, to be able to see an event before we go, puts us at ease and gives us an idea of what to expect.

Your event promo videos should show your event *experience*, rather than showcasing your brand as the event creator. Of course, you can touch on *why* you created the event, but remember that good marketing never centers around you, and neither should a promo. Refer to "How to Read This Book" for a refresher.

Interviews

An interview video is a chance for you to tell people the *why* behind your brand. When these are done right, they help you connect with your audience and talk about your brand's foundation, purpose, and evolution.

Another interview video you could develop could show employees, customers, or friends talking about *why* they are so committed to your brand or business. Interview videos offer a vast array of possibilities. In marketing-speak, we call these *talking head videos*; so, if you've ever heard that term, expect an interview.

Customer Feedback/Testimonials

People believe other people. It's as simple as that. Creating customer video testimonials will go a long way in helping persuade other people to give you a chance. In order to get the best testimonials, be sure you're doing the best work.

Make sure your passion comes through when you're working with people, because passion is contagious, and your customers will remember that when it's time to vouch for you. Your passion will naturally spill over, and their feedback and testimonial will reflect that enthusiasm.

Product or Service Demonstrations

One of my favorite phrases is "I can show you better than I can tell you." Think about that if you're exploring developing a demo video. Your goal here is to walk people through an experience. You want to give people a feel for what it's like to either use your product or services. The focus of a product or service demo video is to provide people step-by-step guidance for how something works.

Case Studies

Case study videos are a great way for brands to showcase their role in ventures and projects. Case study videos show the project before you started, and then walk people through the changes you suggested and led. At the end of these videos, people should have a better idea of how your expertise is of value. For case study videos, the focus is the company or person you helped and how their situation was improved, not your brand.

Teasers

Movies do the best job of teasing content. They drop just enough to make you want to know and see more. That same concept can be applied to brands and businesses. For example, if you're getting ready to launch a new line of products next month, you may want to tease the products with a short snippet of information that gets people excited and eager for their release.

Animation

People love fun cartoon videos because they're lighthearted. These types of videos are great for simplifying complex or difficult topics. Think software programs or educational offerings. Animated videos won't be applicable to every brand, but they are certainly a fun way to show how your brand solves a problem by using cartoon characters to lighten the mood.

Behind-The-Scenes

People love behind-the-scenes video footage because it feels like an inside scoop. They make people feel like they're in the know, so these videos can really attract people to your brand. Think about doing "A Day in the Life" or "My Typical Monday Morning" that shows people a more personal side of who is behind your brand.

Live Videos

Live videos are newer on the scene but are proving to be quite impactful. People like them because they feel more intimate and allow people to ask their questions (and get responses) on the spot. These feel different to people than pre-recorded videos and really bring forth a brand's human side. Use live videos to show people what you're up to at that *exact* moment, but only if it's interesting and fun.

THINGS TO KNOW

You Have About Seven Seconds to Hook People	Keep your videos short, and get to the point quickly. Just because something is in video format doesn't mean people won't close out of it or scroll past it.
Video Titles Matter	Focus less on having a creative or clever title, and instead highlight the key takeaways of the video. Use the title to let people know what you're going to be talking about.
Boring Videos Don't Get Watched	When thinking about the type of video you want to produce, ask yourself if you would watch your entire video. If not, it could probably use some revising and streamlining.

Here are a few final recommendations for developing dynamic brand videos as a part of your marketing strategy.

✓ When you can, invest in a quality videographer or video production agency that has the tools to make your brand look professional. Sure, you can develop videos on your own, but in order for you to be seen as credible, some instances will require you to step things up a bit.

✓ If you post your videos on YouTube, add keywords to help people find your content. Add in a description of your video and include a title, categories, and tags. YouTube has a very sophisticated backend setup, so including this information will help your content show in more places.

✓ Your video should not feel like an advertisement. Focus on being your authentic self in the video. People will respond more favorably.

Wrapping Things Up

When done right, video makes you and your brand a lot more interesting. If you focus on being helpful first and foremost, half of your job is already done.

Video makes people more likely to believe what you're saying and buy into the brand of you.

Remember that video marketing isn't limited to social media. Sure, you can (and should) post your brand videos on YouTube as well as your other favorite social media sites, but also add them to your emails and website.

CHAPTER 10

Email Marketing is Not Dead

Nope, email isn't dead. In fact, it's actually still a very *vital* element in marketing that sets the stage for brands to be more profitable in their long-term ventures, regardless of whether it's a personal brand or business endeavor.

What most people don't know is that email marketing still leads the pack as the **most effective marketing tool** available to brand builders, beating out everything from social media to affiliate marketing.

Email is your opportunity to connect with **masses** of people quickly—meeting them where they are—in their inbox. Email offers you a chance to create personal online networks (beyond social media) of people that support you, wait to hear from you, and become your *tribe* as your brand grows.

WHAT IS A TRIBE?

A tribe is a group of people that advocates for (or keeps up with) your brand or business. They could be customers, email subscribers, social media friends or followers, or anyone that has an interest in the things you do—those people are part of *your* tribe.

The best thing about email is that it provides an entry point for you to have *continued* communication with people. Keyword: continued. That continuance is the key to converting someone's curiosity to currency (and currency [profit] is likely a factor for why you want to improve your marketing).

We're constantly being sold to. All day every day we're being pushed products, ideas, services, upgrades, replacements, substitutions, and resources—each one supposedly better than the last. We get promotions from every direction. We hear ads as we listen to streaming radio or browse websites on our laptops;

we're inundated with commercials on television and sales pitches on social media. It seems like as soon as you get into a groove, boom, it's time to pause for an advertisement you don't even plan on listening to.

Everybody wants something from us, and your brand is no different. Even if you aren't looking for a credit card swipe at that exact moment, there will come a time when you'll be looking to capitalize on the attention of *your* community. And, there's nothing wrong with that.

But we, as humans, have options. Lots of options. So that means that your brand needs to convince people that their money is better spent on you, over someone else essentially doing or selling the same thing.

Sure, you can connect with people through social media, you can even garner some solid business through social channels, but what happens if one day a social media site disappears? It may sound unfathomable, but it can absolutely happen.

You've spent all this time connecting with followers on your social media page, liking posts and pictures; you may have even had small talk a few times, but with the site gone, so are your connections.

Social media sites *own* the contact information of their users, which means that information is their information, not yours. They know who *their* people are, and they know how to reach them if something goes awry; but unfortunately, you don't. Your social connections could be lost at any time. <u>With email marketing, you own your lists</u>—but with social media, you never will.

Oh, and what about hackers? They're everywhere. What if someone hacks your social media brand page, rendering you unable to log back in? What are you going to do? How will you find and reconnect with those people? You'll have to start from scratch.

Not to mention that lookers and likers (as I like to call social media viewers) aren't always easy to convince. Social media is often a starting point where someone becomes familiar with a brand, but all too often, people aren't immediately persuaded to purchase something unknown—especially things with higher price tags like services or expertise. And sure, you have a website, but I guarantee you no one is sitting on it waiting for you to make updates and add new content. Not one person. You have to reach out to people and let them know what's going on with you while connecting it to what's going on with them.

THE ART OF THE ASK

Convincing People to Give You Their Email Address

Getting people to part with their email address is not always the easiest task. People want to know *why* you want it, *what* you plan to do with it, if you plan to share it, *what* you plan to send, and if it'll truly be safe in your hands. Not only do people want to be assured that they won't be inundated with an influx of salesy emails, but they also want to know that what you'll be sending will be interesting and relevant to them. In short, they try to gauge the level of value they think something offers before committing.

This is your time to convince people that emails from you will be nothing short of life-changing. That might be a big ask, but in all seriousness, this is your chance to tell people what they'll get by subscribing to your emails.

Does becoming a subscriber mean they'll get exclusive behind-the-scenes access to your life or business? If so, say that. Will they get tips that help them improve something they're struggling with? If so, elaborate. What about special offers and discounts? What's the incentive? Be sure you clearly state all of the incentives so that people know how they'll benefit from subscribing. This is your chance to *persuade* people. Your goal is to build your roster so that you have instant access to your tribe of people whenever you want.

> **DID YOU KNOW?**
>
> You can also add an option that allows people to subscribe to your emails directly from many social media pages, including Facebook and Pinterest.

I encourage email marketing because it's so inexpensive. For the sake of this discussion, let's just call a spade a spade; it's cheap! Who doesn't love a cheap and effective way to grow a brand? I raise my hand for email marketing every time, for every brand, regardless of your product, service, or business goal—and still, so many brands don't use it.

Think about your best friend. You all catch up on your lives pretty regularly, but you've both been so busy with life stuff that you haven't talked in months. You've been living and learning, and you want to catch them up on so many things. You've lost some weight and want to share the details, you tried some new restaurants that were delicious, you found a new barber or hairstylist that they might like, you just learned about a new show on Netflix that you can't stop binge-watching or you read about certain foods that promote healing. You have updates! And more than likely, your friend does too.

You all need to *communicate*, and when you do get around to checking in with each other, the conversation will flow and be full of eye-opening sharing that refuels you and gives you more to look forward to. Well, email marketing is that best friend.

Email marketing is an opportunity to connect one-on-one with someone while building your credibility at the same time. Think of it as your chance to be personal and personable. You're able to build rapport, help people learn about the things you're an expert on, and become more trustworthy.

QUICK TIP: TIME MATTERS

The time factor is critical. A best practice is to set expectations to your subscribers, letting them know how often they can expect emails from you. Will it be quarterly, monthly, or weekly?

Whatever you decide, let people know the frequency up front. Unless you have a lot of other methods of communicating with your target audience, I'd recommend steering clear of quarterly emails. It's simply not frequent enough. People will likely forget who you are or disengage. Both are harmful to your brand. Consider starting out monthly or biweekly, keeping in mind that you'll need to plan ahead to meet your timelines and stay on track.

Email Compliance:
The Really Important Government Stuff

One thing that is important to know about email marketing is that there are regulations to emailing people on behalf of a brand or business. The most notable are the CAN-SPAM Act (Controlling the Assault of Non-Solicited Pornography and Marketing Act of 2003) and more recently the GDPR (General Data Protection Regulation). Both of these were put in place to ensure businesses are being compliant in emailing people and storing their personal data.

Before you embark on your email endeavors, do some quick research on these two business rules. They're not as scary as they sound. In fact, they really just require businesses to:

> » include a real, physical mailing address in their emails
>
> » offer people an easy way to opt-out and unsubscribe
>
> » offer people the opportunity to update their subscription preferences

Typically, the marketing email software you decide to use to send out your brand's email communications will force you to follow these rules, which means you won't need to spend your time focused on staying compliant.

GETTING STARTED WITH EMAIL MARKETING

Now you're ready to be an email marketing powerhouse. You've determined your focus and your frequency, people are subscribing through your website and social media pages, and now you're ready to talk to your subscribers. But how do you start? It's the same for every brand—it starts with a hello.

FIRST THINGS FIRST:
INTRODUCE YOURSELF

Welcome Your New Subscribers

Your welcome email is essentially you onboarding a new person just as companies do during the hiring process. Your welcome should start with an introduction from you, about you. It's an opportunity for you to introduce yourself to your new friend. Of all the brands in the world, each seeking to be noticed and appreciated, this person made the decision to subscribe to *your* content. It's time to not only say *"hello"* but also say *"thank you."* As the saying goes, <u>you only get one chance to make a first impression, and this is your first impression</u>. For newer brands, this is a good time to briefly share your story.

Let your subscribers know why you do what you do. Tell people how you got into your field and why you're so passionate about it. Focus on making your welcome email human and sincere.

✓ Depending on your brand, you may want to say "thank you" by offering an incentive. For example, a 15% off coupon, a free download, or a tool that helps address a pain point.

✓ As a brand, you never want to make people do the work to find you. Be sure to let people know all the other ways they can stay connected to you, including providing links to all your social pages and channels. Point them exactly where you want them to go.

✓ Be conscious of how soon you respond to your new subscribers. Try to respond within the first 24 hours. That's your best window of opportunity to start forming lasting email friendships.

Depending on the volume of subscribers, you could drive yourself crazy trying to keep up with the welcome responses. I recommend **automating** your welcome email.

Creating auto-response emails is easy and common. It will reduce your stress and save you time. You want to be sure that you don't miss the opportunity to connect with new subscribers at the pivotal time just after they've decided to trust you.

SETTING UP AUTOMATED EMAILS

Companies like MailChimp and Constant Contact have made it easy for anyone to set up automated emails. They have pre-designed templates where you just fill in the set sections, and you're all done.

Doing Regular Email Check-Ins

The welcome emails are done, so what happens next? How do you decide what you're going to talk to your email subscribers about? From this point on you need to continually touch base with these people. These people now make up your tribe.

Failing to do so is a poor representation of your brand's reliability. The good thing is, email marketing doesn't have to be daunting. Start by sharing new content you've created, whether it be videos, podcasts, or blog posts. Beyond that, just start **talking** to your people.

WHAT TO TALK ABOUT

Announce Your Moves

What announcements can you share about yourself, your colleagues, or your brand? Will you be attending an upcoming event? That's an example of something perfect to share in an email to your subscribers. Invite them to attend, and let them know the dates and times you'll be there so that they can find you (should they choose to attend).

Share What's New or Improved in Your World

Emails are a great way to share your brand improvements, additions, or changes. Though your subscribers may not be customers yet, it's likely that they'll become customers the more you engage with them.

Showcase a New Product or Service

Periodically, you will add a new product, service, or resource to your brand's portfolio. It's only natural. Each change you make offers you an opportunity to spotlight them in your email outreach.

Get to Know *Your* People

A great way to start to better understand the wants and needs of your subscribers and customers is to survey them. Your subscribers are your tribe, and every detail that you collect from surveys helps you help them. People love to be heard and voice their opinions, so let your tribe speak.

Create Series Content

Series content means that you're picking a topic or theme and sticking to it for a set number of email sends. Series content creates regularity, and regularity is a key component of demand. Series content is a great idea for any brand, regardless of the industry.

Start by picking a category that relates to something you stand for. From there, identify different things you can highlight within that category. For example, a chef may decide that he wants to highlight various desserts that can be made from eggnog. He may create a series called "Exclusively Eggnog: Creative Desserts to Delight This Holiday."

Before he starts, he would announce the series, and let people know that they can expect eight different recipes over the next two months. His first email might include a recipe on creating eggnog crème brûlée; whereas another email may include eggnog sponge cake. A series offers you a chance to be fun and creative.

Incentivize, Incentivize, Incentivize

We all need a little bit of encouragement from time to time. Offer your tribe special discounts, freebies, and sneak peeks of things you're doing. They'll love it and will feel like they have inside access into a brand they support.

Say Thank You, and Show Your Gratitude

It's important that you always remember that people have choices, and even with all of the choices and options they have, they chose you. Even if they've never spent a dime on your brand, they're engaged in what you do, and that deserves some recognition.

How you show your gratitude is up to you. You just want to let people know you see them, and you're appreciative of their support. Perhaps it's a once a year special thank you email and a chance to connect with you one-on-one.

LET'S TALK GOALS AGAIN

Think back to the "How to Read This Book" introduction. Good marketing never centers around your brand, and the same is true for your email outreach. Your goal for email is primarily to help others. So, with that in mind, focus on sharing your knowledge and expertise, but also start to open up and let your tribe in a bit more than you do the average person. You and your tribe are friends, and friends share.

People need and want things, and thus they seek opportunities to learn from someone who can help. Just as you would help someone in a one-on-one, in-person discussion, you must also seek to provide that same type of support, assistance, and guidance in your emails. But what exactly does that look like?

Here are four examples of how brands can be creative in their email marketing efforts.

Shoe or Clothing Brand	These people likely subscribed because they identify with your brand style. Emails could talk about upcoming shoe designs, pop-up shops, and events. If a certain holiday is coming up, you can suggest shoes or clothes that would be great to have in your closet. You could highlight categories of products (for example: new boots or winter collection). Also, you can share photos of people wearing your shoes that you pull from social media.
Food Service	People likely subscribed because they enjoy food, either eating it or cooking it. Your emails could showcase recipes or tell people about upcoming food specials you'll be offering. If you know from the research you've done in chapter five "What's Brand Growth Without a Strategy?," that your consumers are busy, perhaps your emails will highlight precooked or easy-to-prepare meals.

Health and Wellness	People likely subscribed because they care about their health or physical appearance. Your emails could provide them tips to feel better or look better. Video is also a great way to connect people to your health and wellness brand. See chapter nine, "Using Video to Revolutionize Your Brand." Think about including videos in your actual email sends. Videos in emails improve engagement and shares.
Consulting	These people likely subscribed because they need help with your area of expertise; therefore, your email communication should continually convey that expertise. You could highlight an article or blog post that you recently wrote, let people know about upcoming events you're speaking at, or share best practices in your industry that can help your subscribers become more knowledgable on a specific topic.

Getting More Email Subscribers

In addition to continually communicating with the people that already trust you (your subscribers), you'll want to actively work to grow the number of people in your email list. More people means more possible buyers and brand loyalists. However, convincing people to subscribe isn't always easy.

Here are a few things to help you persuade consumers to let you into their inbox:

- ✓ Give your new subscribers a special offer. It may be a free consult or discounted product or service (like a coupon). People love freebies.

- ✓ Add multiple callouts on your website where you encourage people to subscribe or sign up. Add sign-up details to the end of each article or blog post. Additionally, include sign-up details in the footer of your website and sidebar, if you can. Lastly, add a pop-up subscribe feature that appears to anyone that visits your site.

- ✓ Clearly state what they'll get as a subscriber. An example is "by subscribing to this newsletter, you will receive trend reports and special invites to attend our private events."

✓ Offer a giveaway for anyone who subscribes. Be sure that the giveaway is something that your target consumer will value. See chapter five, "What's Brand Growth Without a Strategy?," referring to the section on determining your target audience. In order to ensure that your incentive will be valuable, you'll need to have a good understanding of what your people are in need of.

✓ Promote your email newsletters or blasts from your social media pages. It's all connected, remember? These days you can link to your email sign-up page directly from many of your social channels.

Wrapping Things Up

Now you're ready to go and flourish with email marketing. A good rule of thumb is to keep your emails informative but relatively short. You don't want to overwhelm people. If you recall, the consumers of today have short attention spans. Have fun, be brief, and be consistent.

CHAPTER 11

Brand Yourself For Demand

Regardless of your industry or goals, having a personal brand can benefit anyone. Plus, with practically everything in society happening online, developing your personal brand has never been more important than it is now. Business is global, which means opportunities exist worldwide. The popularity of social media has closed gaps and connected the world like we've never seen before.

With the tap of a button, we meet new people online and make connections that change the trajectory of our lives. Your personal brand is how you differentiate yourself from others. If you weren't sure before, now is the perfect time to build your online presence as a means of opening new doors.

For business owners, there are massive benefits to building a personal brand in addition to a business brand. For individuals, including consultants and subject matter experts, having a personal brand will help you define your contributions to your industry and set yourself apart. The best part about building your personal brand is that it's really not nearly as hard to create as it sounds.

Before You Begin, Self-Reflect

Before starting the process of building your online prominence, it's important that you self-reflect. Think about who you'd like to become. Then, start identifying people you admire. You're getting ready to step-up your presence, which involves you marketing yourself through a variety of online and social media platforms.

It's time to shift how you think about yourself. For anyone looking to be known in their field or advance in their career, developing a personal brand is a must.

THE BRAND OF YOU:
START HERE

> » Who are you now, and who do you want to transform yourself into?

> » Why are you looking to create your personal brand?

> » Who are you trying to appeal to?

> » What are you the proudest of in your personal and professional life?

> » What do you wish you could redo?

During this phase, every insight helps. Your aha moments will probably come in spurts, followed by lulls. Take it all in stride and use every insight to help you plan, focus, strategize, and visualize your future self.

In-depth self-reflection is a must because it will help you define and tell your personal brand story, and that story is what's going to set you apart from everyone else. Everyone has unique circumstances and situations that make them who they are. Don't be ashamed to share these things; they humanize you and make you more real. They will ultimately be some of the most advantageous things about you. (See chapter six, "Captivate and Connect With Your Brand Story," for a refresher.)

QUICK TIP: YOUR MINDSET MATTERS

Before beginning, it's important to make a mindset shift. First and foremost, you have to realize that **you yourself are a brand**, and that as a brand, you seek to influence other people in some way. Start marketing yourself the same way top influencers and celebrities do. Soon enough, you'll be a big deal.

DISCOVER & DEFINE "YOU THE BRAND"

WHERE YOU ARE VS. WHERE YOU WANT TO BE
THE REINVENTION

Even though you may have already established who you are in your day-to-day life, there will be a rein-vention process as you start to define and develop your public-facing personal brand. One of the easiest ways to start on the path to your defining this is to take inventory. Simply put, that refers to asking the people around you what they think of you. It's important to know how others see you.

Once you get an idea of how you're perceived, you'll be more prepared to address personal gaps (which we all have) and areas of improvement. It's funny because a lot of times people think they know themselves so well, but once they ask for concrete feedback, they're surprised at what they hear.

What you think you're putting out may actually be very different from how people are receiving it. It's important not to be discouraged by what you hear. All of it may not be positive, but it's always constructive—and constructive feedback offers you an opportunity to learn and reflect on how to become a better version of yourself.

One of the easiest ways to get insight on yourself is to talk to your friends and co-workers. They know you personally, they interact with you regularly, and they pay attention to things that you might not even know you do. Set up interviews with these people. They can be formal or informal but will give you dedicated time to ask for concrete feedback. Another good resource is to go and look at your past performance evaluations and job-related feedback to see what your supervisors and colleagues have said about you. Look at how they described and perceived you. Lastly, think about things that people have said to you in general conversation. Use all of these insights and start to dissect yourself so that you have as much background on *you* as possible.

THE "ME BRANDING ME" INTERVIEW PROCESS

More affectionately known as the "you branding you" interview process.

Start by asking the people in your life to give you three to five words they would use to describe you. Then, have them go through each word and elaborate on why they chose it. Ask for specific examples from past experiences with you.

Also, ask each person what they think you're good at. You're looking to hear what they think are your strengths? Then, follow up by asking what they see as your weaknesses.

FEEDBACK IS HELPFUL WHETHER IT'S POSITIVE OR NOT-SO-POSITIVE

One of my favorite sayings is *you don't know what you don't know.* A lot of people have a tough time being reviewed or assessed, especially if the feedback is not favorable. Although hearing feedback isn't always easy, it's always helpful. Don't look at negative feedback as a personal attack. Instead, look at it as something that was shared to help you grow.

Understand that everyone has limitations and short-comings. It's important to remember that even if you hear not-so-pleasant things about yourself, this insight will ultimately only help you become a better you.

SEARCH YOURSELF ON SEARCH ENGINES

Once you've finished your interviews, next up are search engines. It's time to search yourself on the web. What's currently showing up under your name? Start with Google, then once you've thoroughly searched the results, move on to sites like Bing and Dogpile.

Different search engines often contain different details, so it's good to cover all your bases. You may need to reach out to sites to have erroneous or inappropriate information removed, but it's worth the effort as you start to craft your personal brand. We're talking about *you* the brand after all. You want things to be accurate and best reflect who you are looking to shift into.

DID YOU KNOW?

In addition to searching your name by typing first followed by last, try searching for your name in quotation marks. Often that will bring up different results, and the more thorough your search of yourself, the more likely you are to cover all your bases.

Building Your Personal Brand Narrative

Because no two people are the same, no two brands are alike. That's especially true for personal brands. Even people that have the same careers or passions have different backstories, different personalities, and different goals. That right there is enough to make your narrative unique.

Before you embark on the journey of building your personal brand and narrative, you have to do three main things:

(1) believe that good outcomes are possible
(2) be willing to learn
(3) continually strive to reach new goals

A QUICK MINDSET CHECK

Believe.

Our thoughts are a funny thing. There have been countless studies that show that your thoughts actually shape your reality. Negative thinking yields negative outcomes. So, it's important for you to remain optimistic even though you can't yet see the end result.

Optimism doesn't mean that you don't worry or doubt yourself, it just means that negativity is not your dominant thought. It's important to remember that your thoughts are a living, breathing thing—so when you think about energy and frequency—believing in positive outcomes is essential to seeing positive outcomes.

Be willing to learn.

Not just in brand building, but in life, you must be willing and open to learning new things—and learning them constantly. The beauty of living is the opportunity for lifelong learning. That includes picking up new skills, staying informed of new and emerging trends in your field, and seeking opportunities to connect with people smarter than you or who have different perspectives than you. All of this will strengthen your brand in the long run, not to mention it will make you more interesting to engage with and talk to.

Continually strive to reach new goals.

Everything you do in your quest to build your personal brand won't stick. What does that mean exactly? It means that not all of your efforts will give you the results you're hoping for. That's not a time to get discouraged, but rather an opportunity for you to showcase your resilience. The strongest, most successful figures have faced adversity and major setbacks, but what sets them apart is their determination to continually adjust and change their goals if something doesn't work.

> ## WHERE TO START: DEFINE WHAT YOU WANT YOUR BRAND TO BE
>
> Pull your notes from chapter four, "Where You Fit In: Defining Your Brand," as you'll need them to develop your personal brand. Your personal brand is an opportunity for you to showcase more than your business talents. It's also your chance to showcase your personality and personal interests. Have fun with it!

THINKING DIGITALLY

TIME TO CURATE YOUR ONLINE PRESENCE

Get yourself a website.

Having a personal website is one of the most effective tools to market yourself and your business. Buy your name or some fancy iteration of who you seek to be in your industry. Your personal brand website URL could be *www.alanajames.com* or *www.alanathechef.com*. It's up to you.

Align your social sites to your personal brand.

Because social media is so influential in personal brand success, it's important that you tie them to your brand. Link your social pages from your personal website (as long as they are representative of your brand experience).

You may not feel comfortable linking every social media site you're on to your public-facing personal brand, and that's fine. Perhaps you may only want to align LinkedIn and Twitter, and exclude Instagram and Facebook because they are more personal. That's okay, but think about creating brand-facing versions of those pages as well. It's more for you to manage but will offer you additional exposure and more opportunity.

Share your thoughts.

People aren't mind readers. Before people buy into your brand, they want to get an idea of your mindset. The best way to share your thoughts is through content. Revisit chapter seven, "Craft Your Content Like a Boss," to make sure you're developing and sharing content that will most effectively get you to your goals.

Wrapping Things Up

If you don't create your own brand narrative, you leave the door open for others to do it for you.

Building your personal brand sets the stage for opportunities to find you. Develop the brand of you and attract a wealth of new engagements. If you are also a business owner, having a personal brand that ties into your business brand is a great way to show the human behind the business.

PART 4

Build Your Community

CHAPTER 12

Collaboration is the New Competition

I t's a shame how many people are afraid of working with others in their industry (or simply other people in general). I can't tell you how many executives and entrepreneurs I meet that don't want to collaborate because they see someone as competition. Working with other people can open up a wealth of opportunities and usher in new networks of people that can turn into some of your most profitable partnerships.

Bill Nye (as in Bill Nye, the Science Guy) once said: "Everyone you meet knows something you don't."

When we don't see someone as competition, we love sharing ideas. It's our thing. We open up and talk, suggest, reveal, laugh, ponder, guide and divulge. We're open and communicative, even vulnerable. But for some strange reason, when we see someone as competition, even if they were once a close friend, we shut down and close-up, generally because we're either subconsciously threatened that their genius will infringe on our genius, or we're worried that our ideas will be stolen and used without us.

When someone is our competition, they are a *threat.*

Our mind says: my ideal customer only has a specific amount of money to spend, and if someone else does the same thing as me, I can't be sure the opportunity will present to me.

We become more protective of our brands and seek to differentiate ourselves further, but big wins can be found by collaborating with your friends as well as the people you see as competitors.

Chances are you're not a multibillion-dollar brand yet. If you are, kudos, and well done. You're a brand powerhouse. However, if you haven't reached billionaire status yet, definitely start collaborating now.

COMPETITION IS ALL IN HOW YOU FRAME IT

When competition is turned into collaboration, everybody wins, especially small or start-up brands that are typically focused on growing awareness and getting in front of more people. The exchange of ideas fosters growth unlike anything you could ever imagine.

THE POWER OF COLLECTIVE IDEATION

When I say "collective ideation," I mean many minds and ideas coming together with their creativity and varied strengths. You may be highly-analytical and creative but not so good with selling and pitching your ideas. Collaborating with other people allows you to leverage their strengths and vice versa. It also helps you identify more potential obstacles up front so that you are better able to cover your bases when planning for things like product launches and brand expansion projects.

Have you ever heard the phrase: "Ideas grow when they are shared?" Looking at top brands and businesses, you'll notice one thing they all have common— the frequency of brainstorming sessions. Brainstorming sessions are collective ideation exemplified. They're a meeting of the minds where openness is encouraged and celebrated.

Use this same collaborative concept when you think about your brand. Brainstorming sometimes bring out outlandish ideas, which is honestly a great thing. Those are the ones you want to hear. The crazier the better. The biggest and boldest ideas often feel impossible at first. So, as your passion and purpose unite, remember that just because an idea isn't possible at the present time doesn't mean it's not worth exploring for the future. Write down every idea and revisit them in a year. You never know, that idea might be perfect 12-24 months from now.

A COMMON GOAL

Find someone whos ambition aligns with yours. They don't need to have the same brand or business goals as you; they simply need to be working towards something greater than where they are now, just as you are. They need to have a big vision just as you do.

They can be in a different region, industry, age group, or social circle. If you can see some alignment (any alignment) in connecting your brands, major things can begin to take shape once you start collaborating.

Here's an example:

A fitness enthusiast and financial advisor meet at a networking event. They're both in the process of building their personal brands and are looking to increase their networks. They may decide to throw an event together called "Fitness and Financial Freedom: Lose Weight, Save More, and Own Your Happiness." Initially, there weren't any similarities in their brands, but with a little creativity and collaboration, new ideas undoubtedly emerge.

Overcoming Obstacles

One of the best things about collaboration is that it comes with a built-in accountability partner. That partner will help you stay motivated and stay on your path because your success is intricately tied to their success. There will be days when self-doubt slips in and you question your journey. When you're working with someone else, they can help lift your spirits when you're overwhelmed, feeling low, or questioning your direction. Additionally, they can serve as a mentor, confidant, or simply a listening ear that helps ease the stress while you find your voice and discover your genius.

Even after you've taken the deep dive to build your brand, doubt and fear will still peek in from time-to-time. Questions like "Am I good enough?" or "Does anyone care about what I have to say?" will rear their ugly heads. Every time doubt presents, you have to rise up and *intentionally* shut it down.

Having good accountability partners can really help you out when you question your readiness or worthiness. You're working on something that everyone won't be able to see or understand early on. Forge forward with your likeminded group of go-getters because yes, you can become and build the brand you seek to see in the world.

TAKE SOME RISKS

Without risk, your rewards will always be limited. In order to build a successful brand, you can't always play it safe. You have to be willing to go blindly into the unknown to obtain the lifestyle you seek. Risk can be hard for some people to get the hang of, so collaborating is a good way to ease the angst of risk-taking because you have a built-in sounding board that is familiar with your challenges and struggles and thus helps you stay the course to your greater path. Remember that risk is not a bad thing and shouldn't steer you away from pursuing your brand goals.

Just because an idea hasn't yet taken shape doesn't mean you can't create something monumental. Collaboration + passion + creativity can equal massive success. Just look at Facebook. A group of college friends came together and launched what was to become the most successful social networking site in history. If this isn't enough to convince you to collaborate and go against the norm, I don't know what else to say.

Wrapping Things Up

Let your guard down, and let people in. Tap into the brainpower of like-minded people to help you get past the things you see as challenges. They'll also be there to motivate you to show up on when you don't feel like it. Connect with other passionate and focused people and watch how your ideas flourish. The enthusiasm that your collective group feels will rise to the surface and usher in new ways of thinking. Link your brands together, get creative and go make magic happen.

CHAPTER 13

People Trust You. Now What?

Once you get to this stage, let me be the first to tell you—you're officially in a relationship. Your brand has pledged and committed to love, support, and honor *your* people (also known as your tribe) for the foreseeable future. If you thought growing your audience meant you were done, I'm so sorry to break it to you, but that's simply not the case. It's only the beginning to your happily ever after.

The good thing is, your brand is growing. People see the value of your expertise and skills and are starting to become more familiar with who you are, what you stand for, and the things your brand represents. People enjoy the experience of you and are telling others about you. **But what happens next?**

I've seen so many brands stop there. They take all those interactions and connections and they either do nothing, or they disappear. They essentially abandon their tribes until they need them again. They don't reach out or stay in touch until it's time to sell another product or service, and this is a major brand no-no.

Consumers, followers, customers and social media friends alike can feel that lack of connectedness, and they don't appreciate it. They invested in you after all, and in doing so, expect you to continue to remain present and at minimum continue talking to them.

How would you feel if you were dating someone, then all of a sudden, they turned off their phone, disappeared, and didn't reach out for three months? That's not okay, right? Exactly, because that's not how relationships work. Whether you want to think about it like that or not, that's exactly what your brand is in. In relationships, seemingly insignificant gestures go a long way in keeping your partner happy, committed, and invested in you.

Think back to when you first started dating and your partner was always available. They'd regularly call and text to see how your day went and you'd get updates on their days as well. You felt connected. Then one day you decided to take your relationship up a notch, splurging, getting the two of you tickets on a cruise getaway. You both raved about the great time you had and started planning future events like concerts and dinner dates but as soon as you got back home, they were ghost. It's been months, and you haven't heard a peep from them. No more check-ins or calls; just straight silence. You're confused and feel the void of them being gone. That's the brand dilemma in relationship terms.

QUICK TIP: SUCCESSFUL BRANDS DON'T ABANDON PEOPLE

Abandonment is the most frequent problem brands (of all sizes) do that negatively impacts their longevity and growth. Most commonly abandonment is the result of limited time or resources, however, tribes, customers, and followers don't understand that. Know that even the smallest of gestures matters. A quick one-paragraph hello email or short video on social media can help close a void.

How would you feel if your partner just up and disappeared? You think they forgot about you, but then three months later out of nowhere, they email and say "hey, how have you been?" To top it off, there was no mention of the disappearing act. The nerve of them right? Well, this is how so many brands operate. They don't **nurture** their relationships. They have the initial interaction, and things are great, but then they disappear for months. I know brands that have disappeared on their customers for over six months, and then came back and asked them to pay and renew their membership, attend a conference or buy a product.

What does that say to people about your brand?

Honestly, it says you don't *really* care about them, and it often says you're only invested when you're looking for a swipe of their credit cards. If you're not concerned with them, why should they be concerned with you?

In relationships, communication is the glue that keeps people connected. When communication is lacking, there's a big void and resentment typically forms as a result. Just as in relationships, resentment can build up, and it will impact how people think about you and how much they are willing to invest in your brand.

DISAPPEARING FOR TOO LONG WILL HURT YOU

The strongest, most successful brands engage in frequent communication with their tribes. As such, they form bonds long-term relationships with their people that are sustained as they evolve.

NURTURING YOUR TRIBE

Just as in relationships, people need (and expect) frequent interaction from the brands they support. The more you communicate, the more your tribe will have your back. People will start to rally around your brand and seek you out when they need a problem solved.

But, what's the best way to go about nurturing your customers? Either start talking or start by typing. Enter emails, social media content, or video. It's impossible to check-in with every member of your tribe one-on-one; however, you will need to get in the habit of periodically checking in where the majority of your people are.

Interact With Them Through Social Media

Social interaction can be something as simple as posting a picture or video. Maybe you'd prefer to start a conversation for your community to chime in on. Sometimes you may want to share your opinion on a recent event and ask what your people think. Interactions matter. Share your thoughts, ideas, tips, concerns or stance on something as a way to open the door for information exchanges.

Do Quick Check-Ins

A simple "how are things going" goes a long way. Say it's been a month since your last virtual chat. Send them a quick email, direct message or post saying hello, and ask them to update you on something you previously chatted about.

STAY IN YOUR TRIBE'S INBOX

Use your email communication as an opportunity to stay connected to your tribe. Talk to them about *them*, and then talk to them about *you*. As in any relationship, it's important to provide emotional support as well as sharing what's going on in your world.

If you're working on something new, these are the people that should know about it first. These are your people. If you're planning to be at an exhibit or conference, let them know about it ahead of time. Not only will they possibly show up, but they may tell other people about it as well. They'll say, "this is my favorite brand because they always keep me in the loop."

Show People You Remember Them

If someone learned about your brand because they needed help for a specific problem, that's your hook (at least a good place to start). Say you own a spa and a customer came to you because they were struggling with skin discoloration and breakouts. Your brand helped them reduce the oil in their skin, so when you go back to talk to them again, make this the focus of your conversation. You could lead with something about acne remedies as the seasons change. That helps the consumer solve a problem while positioning you as an expert on the topic.

Ask Them for Feedback

Tell your tribe you want their opinion on something. Perhaps you're working on a new product or partnership and want to know if they would prefer one option over another. Asking them for feedback will help keep them engaged, while also providing you valuable intel into what your tribe is *ultimately* looking for.

BUILD A COMMUNITY FOR YOUR TRIBE

Note that this does not say "build your community." Building a community means that you have a place where your tribe can come and connect with each other and share ideas, discuss challenges, and network. So, for clarity: community is the place, and your tribe are the people.

The benefit of this community is (1) it's under your brand umbrella, so you're the convener that provides the value, and (2) you'll be able to get an inside look at what your tribe is talking about. You'll have your pulse on your community by seeing what your people are talking about.

All of these will help you make smarter decisions about the things you produce for your brand. Additionally, this allows your customers to generate their own content, which reduces the amount of work you have to do—and who doesn't want that?

The easiest place to build your community is on your website or through a social media platform like Facebook. An easy way to build your community is to create a Facebook group. That will then become a place where your people can log in and link up.

Also, as your email list grows, you can email people updates on what's happening in your community and encourage them to invite others to join.

DATA COLLECTION:
ANALYZING YOUR METRICS

What are metrics? Metrics are measurements. They are **your brand stats**, and they tell you what's working and not working with regards to your marketing. A key ingredient in the secret sauce of great marketing is **measurement**. Metrics are not the most glamorous part of marketing, but they're the things that will prevent you from wasting your time and money in the long-run.

All good marketers use metrics and data to improve profit, increase engagement, and close more deals. So, what that means is, in order to build a successful brand, you'll need to start familiarizing yourself with marketing metrics and brand data.

Knowing Your Brand Data is Important

Think about metrics as intelligence that will help you improve what you develop in the future. This could include the types of photos you take and post, the videos you create, the emails you send, and even how your website is designed. Data is everywhere, and it's not as hard to pull information as you think.

Here is a quick list of basic data points that you can start pulling.

THINGS YOU SHOULD KNOW

RE: Your Website Stats

✓ How many website visitors do you get each month?

✓ What are the top 3-5 web pages people go to?

✓ Where are your site visitors from?
Which states or countries do you see most frequently represented?

✓ Which web pages are your most visited?
Knowing your top content is important because that determines where you should promote your services and new products.

✓ How long do people typically stay on your website? [Duration]

If the amount of time that people stay on your website is short, then you might need to change up the wording or content to get site visitors to stay and look around longer.

✓ How are people getting to your website?

Are more people finding you through search engines or social media? Knowing how people locate you will help you better identify which types of content work best.

SET UP GOOGLE ANALYTICS

For your website, be sure you have Google Analytics set up on the back end so that you know which of your pages are the most visited. This also helps you understand where people are (and aren't) going once they get to your website. Knowing the things people aren't doing is often more beneficial than knowing the things they are doing. Perhaps you think that the majority of your website traffic is visiting your services page, when in fact, most visitors never go to that page. This insight can help you start figuring out your brand whys and allow you to make adjustments and increase profit and sustainability.

RE: Your Email Marketing Stats

✓ How many people are opening your emails compared to the number of people you send emails to?

✓ Of the people that open your emails, how many of those people actually click through and read the content on your website? Then, of the people that click through to your website, how many take action (e.g., send you a message, comment on a post, download a resource, or buy a product)?

✓ What types of subject lines get the most email opens?

✓ What gets more email opens? Emails that you send in the morning, or those you send in the afternoon? Does sending an email on a Tuesday get you more opens than sending it on a Thursday? Often, the day you send an email matters.

Knowing the details of your email outreach will help you develop better email communications in the future that get higher open and click rates. Also, better emails mean less unsubscribes and more brand loyalty.

RE: Your Social Media Stats

✓ Which types of posts have the most engagement?
  Engagement may present as likes, comments, shares, or direct messages.

✓ Which captions generate the most discussions, comments, or shares?

✓ Which content captures the most attention?
  Words or quotes, photos, videos, or something else.

Look for trends. Knowing your numbers means that you can make improvements and be better at planning out your marketing efforts and creating more interesting content. Check your data frequently, even if you can only take 15 minutes a week. Every nugget of knowledge helps.

Wrapping Things Up

As a brand, it's important for you to *own* the conversation around who you are and what you stand for by doing regular check-ins on your tribe. **And yes, you actually have to talk to them (not at them).** Effective nurturing combined with knowing your metrics will help you form lifelong connections with your tribe.

CONCLUSION

Final Thoughts

Pull up a chair.

Grab your notebook, and write down all the things you want your brand to embody.

Identify who *you* are.

Envision your future self.

Then rise to become that person.

If you know nothing else, know that it's all worth it. Every bit of angst you feel is worth it in your quest to be your own brand, business, and ultimately your own boss.

It starts with you saying it. You have to claim it. We each have a path that is tied to our gifts and interests, but the only way to get it is to leave your comfort zone and begin to embrace your evolution.

The best parts of life are lined in uncertainty. Behind the door of your successful brand is the biggest gem you could ever imagine for yourself—freedom. Freedom to live your life on your terms and the courage to follow your passion. When you commit to this process and have a powerful desire to make things happen, absolutely anything is possible.

Continually marketing yourself, your brand, and your business will be vital from now on. In the "How to Read This Book" opener, I started out saying "good marketing never centers around you." You're simply a vessel of help to someone else. Your biggest asset (and most profit) will come from positioning your talents and expertise as something that is of aid and assists others. How do you help people step into their potential, be happier, be more empowered or be more confident?

Social media and online marketing are your friends. They offer enormous opportunities for brand awareness because they connect with millions of people instantly (and globally). You'll need to be intentional about everything you do for your brand from now on. Make sure your brand is cohesive across all of your platforms. That means that if you use a certain set of colors and fonts on your website, those same colors and fonts should be in your email outreach, social media, and brand collateral like business cards and brochures.

As you read through this book, hopefully you identified some areas where you can streamline or adjust how you communicate to be more effective in marketing yourself. Once you define how your brand addresses consumers' problems, you're halfway there.

More than anything else, your brand should be the thing that helps people think differently and see themselves in a new light. Focus on inspiration, motivation and education for maximum impact. Remember that marketing is not just promotion; there are so many other elements to consider beyond just the advertising and sales components of brand building.

You may be the underdog right now, but with the right strategy and plan for success, that will all change. Being open to learning and listening will help you continually evolve your brand. Listen to everything your [ideal] consumers do and say. If you're having a conversation in person, listen to their pain points and struggles (and make sure your brand addresses them). If you're on social media, watch what your target consumers are posting and talking about. All of these things matter. All of these will be the things that help you rally a tribe of people that are in your corner as your brand evolves. Your tribe will grow the more you listen and address their needs.

Above all else, remember that creativity is the backbone of successful marketing. No one ever changed the game by doing what everyone else is doing. Work on expanding your presence, gaining trust, and being consistent.

Build your portfolio. Connect and build relationships frequently. Set and track your metrics. Think big.

Marketing can be overwhelming and is certainly a very complex profession. If you didn't know before reading this book, I hope you see now that marketing is much more than one-off promotions. Continue to seek guidance, read a variety of resources, and keep good people in your corner that you can bounce your ideas off of. Effective marketing first requires you to build an authentic, credible, and memorable brand. Now's the time!

YOU CAN ABSOLUTELY BUILD A HIGHLY SUCCESSFUL, CRAVED BRAND.

Applying the Lessons in This Book to Your Brand [Q&A]

It's time to identify your passion. What are you passionate about, and why?

_____

_____

If you're unsure about your passion, start instead by thinking about things you truly enjoy doing. What are some things you love doing?

_____

_____

Consumer Mindset Exercise

Think about yourself as a consumer for a moment.

What kind of consumer are you?

_____ Impatient

_____ Informed

_____ Connected

_____ Self-Aware

_____ Easily Turned Off

How do you most display these behaviors when you shop? (Either in-person or online).

_____

_____

Has a business ever done something that bothered you to the point that you stopped shopping there? What was it that stopped you from continuing as a patron?

(e.g. bad customer service, not keeping promises, hidden costs, inaccessibility). These are the qualities you don't want associated with your brand.

_____

_____

What are some of your favorite brands and why?

What makes them stand out in your mind? The goal here is to think about the elements of that brand that you can pull into your own brand.

_____

_____

Identify a brand that you think has excellent customer service. What about that brand showcases a committment to meeting customer expectations?

_____

_____

About Your Goals

What goals do go you seek to achieve within the next 6-12 months?

(Short-term goals.)

_____

_____

_____

What goals do go you seek to achieve within the next 5-10 years?
(Long-term goals.)

_____

_____

_____

_____

_____

About Your Brand

What made you decide to create your brand? (What's your why?)

_____

_____

_____

_____

_____

What is your brand's core mission?
(What do you do?)

_____

_____

_____

What is your vision for your brand?

_____

_____

_____

_____

Who is your target audience (and why)?

_____

_____

_____

_____

What problem does your brand solve?
(How do you *help* people?)

_____

_____

_____

_____

_____

Why should people trust you to provide
what they're looking for?
(Credibility and expertise.)

_____

_____

_____

_____

_____

What makes your brand different?
(Differentiation.)

_____

_____

_____

_____

Growing Your Credibility

Identify three personal accomplishments
that tie in with your expertise.
(Trainings, school, certifications, years in the field,
notable people you've worked with or for, awards,
recognition.)

a. _____

_____

b. _____

_____

c. _____

_____

Identify three companies, brands, or individuals that you can collaborate or volunteer with (in the next 90 days).

    a. _____

       _____

    b. _____

       _____

    c. _____

       _____

Identify three people that would be willing to vouch for your work and provide you a testimonial.
(Past clients, supervisors, colleagues.)

    a. _____

       _____

    b. _____

       _____

    c. _____

       _____

You (As a Customer)

What matters most to you as a customer?

____ I need to trust the person I'm paying or listening to

____ I like to be able to find someone at a business to talk to (either by phone, internet/email, or face-to-face)

____ I like when businesses send me suggestions for things that I need or have an interest in

____ I like when brands clearly explain the benefits of something to me

____ I like when someone keeps their promises

The things that matter to you should be incorporated into your brand.

Managing Customer Expectations

How will people contact you?
(Website form, social media, etc.)

_____

_____

_____

How will you handle an unhappy customer?

_____

_____

_____

How quickly after a customer (or potential customer) contacts you can they expect a response?

_____

_____

_____

Showcasing Your Brand's Value

What three types of content will you infuse into your brand to showcase your expertise? (e.g. blog posts, articles, interviews, photos, case studies, webinars, etc.)

a. _____

b. _____

c. _____

What social media sites will you use to start to position your brand (and why)?
(e.g. Facebook, Instagram, LinkedIn, Twitter, You-Tube, etc.)

a. _____

b. _____

c. _____

What three personal stories can you tell to show the person behind your brand?

a. _____

_____

b. _____

_____

c. _____

_____

If you decided to develop videos for your brand, what three types would you do, and what would be the focus?

a. _____

_____

b. _____

_____

c. _____

_____

Resources

Chapter 2

SmartInsights.com. "Search Engine Statistics 2018." January 30, 2018. https://www.smartinsights.com/search-engine-marketing/search-engine-statistics/

The New York Times. "The Eight-Second Attention Span." January 22, 2016. https://www.nytimes.com/2016/01/22/opinion/the-eight-second-attention-span.html

Chapter 8

Statista: The Statistics Portal. "Percentage of U.S. population with a social media profile from 2008 to 2018." https://www.statista.com/statistics/273476/percentage-of-us-population-with-a-social-network-profile/

Chapter 9

Forbes. "Top 10 Video Marketing Trends And Statistics Roundup 2017." September 22, 2017. https://www.forbes.com/sites/tjmccue/2017/09/22/top-10-video-marketing-trends-and-statistics-roundup-2017/#5cce0f787103

Forbes. "Survey: YouTube Is America's Most Popular Social Media Platform." March 23, 2018. https://www.forbes.com/sites/meganhills1/2018/03/23/social-media-demographics/#10ab1444783a

BrandWatch. "122 Amazing Social Media Statistics and Facts." January 2, 2019. https://www.brandwatch.com/blog/amazing-social-media-statistics-and-facts/

Chapter 10

SmartInsights.com. "Email marketing is still worth taking seriously in 2018." https://www.smartinsights.com/email-marketing/email-communications-strategy/email-markeing-still-worth-taking-seriously-2018/ February 18, 2018.

Acknowledgments

Wow! I'm officially a published author. Pinch me because I have to be dreaming. As I wrote this book, I reflected on my lineage. I thought about my ancestors who walked a path very different than mine. I stand on the shoulders of their sacrifices, so first and foremost, I dedicate this book to them. Their strength lives in me. I am my ancestors' wildest dreams.

To each and every person that took the time to read this book, a very special thank goes to you. Deserving of special acknowledgment are my clients, past employers, mentors, advisors, customers, colleagues, and friends.

To my parents, Denise and Kelvin, who have always encouraged me to live life on my terms, I love you more than you could ever know. To Grandpa George, Grandpa Cordy, Grandma Margaurita, and Grandma Anita—thank you for your continuous love, support, and frankly, for the best hugs any granddaughter could ask for.

Deserving of special mention is Temple University's Klein College of Media and Communication, specifically all the folks in the advertising department. It is impossible to count all the ways that Temple U (and its outstanding professors) helped shape my life and my career.

To my former ASCO co-workers: Vicki V., Lynne B., Lisa J., and Julie L.—thank you so much for believing in and trusting me to help your lines of business shine. You all taught me so many valuable business skills.

To Catherine 'Cat' Kennedy, I owe you a great debt of gratitude. My sincerest of thank yous for your ongoing input, guidance, support, and sound judgment. You've played a huge part in easing my angst during this journey.

To Jacqueline Loweree, whose belief in this project was unwavering—you are a godsend! To Victoria S. M., Lynnea G., and Antoine S.—you all have always been in my corner (always!), so thank you for being my lifelong motivators. You mean so much to me.

Last, but certainly not least, I am indebted to the talents of Rashad Mohammed of Ram Creates for all of his artistic efforts including the illustration and graphic design of this book. You really bought my ideas to life, and I am eternally grateful.

About the Author

[In her own words.]

Hi, my name is Keli Hammond, and I am the author of this book. My 15 years of marketing industry experience, combined with decades of consulting and coaching everyone from start-up entrepreneurs to fortune 500 executives, has allowed me the unique insights that I share with you in this book.

I was introduced to the world of marketing when I interned at Comcast-Spectacor, a major corporation in the sports and entertainment industry. There, I worked on projects supporting the Philadelphia 76ers, Flyers, and Disney on Ice. After that, I went on to work in management with a variety of companies, both at for-profit companies and non-profit organizations. I even did a brief stint on Wall Street. There, I learned how corporate businesses operate and strategically position themselves for upward mobility and continuous growth.

After New York, I led the marketing efforts for organizations focused primarily on increasing market share, sales volume, and customer retention. Additionally, I helped companies strategically position their brands for expansion to international regions. These projects sent me to Brazil, The Netherlands, Austria, Japan, and Spain, to name a few.

My greatest accomplishments, however, are the awards that I've been so honored to receive: "Best Online Campaign" from the International Advertising Competition and "Digital and New Media Content Merit Winner" from the Healthcare Advertising Awards.

After that, I moved into leadership, helping organizations implement a variety of marketing and strategic change strategies before starting my own boutique branding agency, B Classic. Now, I spend my days consulting and coaching executives, entrepreneurs, and business owners looking to increase their visibility, improve the effectiveness of their marketing, streamline their business ideas, or reinvent themselves.

I earned a BA in Advertising from Temple University (go Owls!) and hold a certificate in Change Leadership from Cornell University.

In my spare time, you'll likely find me on a plane headed to a different part of the world. I've had the pleasure of visiting over 35 countries and always have more on my radar.

I also like coffee, fitness, reading, and salsa dancing. I live in the Washington Metro Area most the time but frequently travel to the New York City area, as I consider it my second home.

Made in the
USA
Middletown, DE

75439346R00182